The Unpast:
The Actual Unconscious

The Unpast:
The Actual Unconscious

by Dominique Scarfone

New York:
The Unconscious in Translation

Copyright © 2015 by The Unconscious in Translation
1050 Fifth Avenue, New York, NY 10028
ucsintranslation@gmail.com
All rights reserved.
First Edition

"A Matter of Time: Actual Time and the Production of the Past" was originally published in Psychoanalytic Quarterly, 75: 807–834, 2006; "Repetition: Between Presence and Meaning" was originally presented at the 45th Congress of the International Psychoanalytic Association, Berlin, 27 July 2007; "In the Hollow of Transference: The Analyst's Position Between Activity and Passivity" was originally published in Sitegeist, 4: 7–20, 2010; "The Unpast: The Actual Unconscious" was originally published as *L'impassé, actualité de l'inconscient*, by Presses Universitaires de France in *Revue française de psychanalyse*, 2014/5 Vol. 78, p. 1357-1428.

ISBN 978-1-942254-07-2
Library of Congress Control Number: 2015957530

> This ISBN is for the paperback
> Create separate layout for this page for Hardcover edition
> ISBN 978-1-942254-06-5

CONTENTS

Foreword • vii

A Matter of Time • 1

Repetition: Between Presence and Meaning • 31

In the Hollow of Transference • 53

The Unpast • 69

Bibliography • 173

Index • 181

Foreword

Time was a somewhat neglected theme in Freud's nearly fifty-year long study of the unconscious, and he himself deplored this fact in one of his late works:

> "Again and again I have had the impression that we have made too little theoretical use of [the] fact, established beyond any doubt, of the unalterability by time of the repressed. This seems to offer an approach to the most profound discoveries. Nor, unfortunately, have I myself made any progress here."[1]

One can only speculate about where a renewed effort on Freud's part would have led him regarding the "unalterability by time of the repressed." In the present series of essays, that idea is embraced again, though from a different angle. Instead of subscribing to the general notion of "timelessness" regarding the unconscious, I take stock of Freud's formulation in the citation above. The "unalterability by time of the repressed" points at something more dynamic or more dialectical than the blunt assertion that the unconscious is timeless. Indeed, if the unconscious were timeless, one might well wonder how any part of it could be brought into a time-bound form of existence. Timelessness points to an unconscious that is out of this world, whereas "the unalterability by time of the repressed," suggests a different story: time does exist for the unconscious, but somehow the repressed is protected from its corrosive effects. The question then becomes what makes the repressed so sturdy?

---

1 Freud (1933 [1932]), Lecture XXXI, SE XXII, p. 74. Translation modified.

To answer this question, rather than take up all that was written on the subject by post-Freudian authors, I chose to go back to basics and to follow a new path through Freud's opus, starting from the foundational works, such as the Project, and going through the early clinical papers and then on to the later writings. Following that path, my attention was caught by the distinction Freud made between the "psychoneuroses of defense" and the ones he called "actual neuroses". The term "actual" struck me because though Freud used the term to qualify the neuroses he thought were not amenable to psychoanalysis, he nevertheless had to admit that he could not erect a definite border between the two kinds of neuroses. Therefore he had no way of keeping the actual neuroses out of the psychoanalytic clinical field; on the contrary, he acknowledged that the psychoneuroses contain a kernel of actual neurosis.

Looking closer, I realized that the relationship existing between "actual" and "defense" neuroses follows a more general pattern that runs throughout the whole Freudian theorization. What is more, the general paradigm that thus emerged rests not so much on topography, which Freud always said was a metaphor, but on a *temporal* basis. I was therefore again drawn to give priority to the dimension of time. I started from the intuition that the word "actual" in "actual neuroses" had to be read through the prism of translation. Indeed, while the English "actual" qualifies something real or concrete, its deceivingly similar German cousin "aktual" belongs to the time dimension, defining that which happens *presently*. Thus, "Aktualneurosen" was a name for neurotic states that had their source in a currently active physiological disturbance rather than in a complex history of trauma, defense, return of the repressed, and so on. Then again, it is not difficult to envisage that what is "actual" in the English sense of real must belong to a present state of affairs and hence the time dimension is never out of view. The "aktual" (presently active) factor invoked by Freud is also "actual" (real) in the English sense of the adjective, and *vice versa*.

But if such an "actual" kernel is at the heart of the psychoneuroses, how can this be reconciled with the so-called timelessness of the unconscious? If what lies at the core is both "actual" (real) and "aktual" (presently active), could we consider that the word and the concept correspond to the state of the repressed that makes it impervious to the passage of time? Following this line of thinking, can we postulate that the unconscious is not so much timeless as it is "actual," in the sense that it is both effectively real and that its time is always "now"? This hypothesis seems promising both theoretically and clinically.

At the *theoretical* level, it serves to protect metapsychology from the metaphysical temptation of referring to metaphorical regions, such as those found in the topographic and structural models, as concrete entities. For while Freud always insisted that although useful these terms must be considered as fictions, our daily parlance has a tendency to reify the psychic "regions" rather than deal with the processes that are the real thing. For instance, working from a mainly temporal point of view we could be spared sterile debates about mechanisms related to the topography of the mind.[2] In practice, psychoanalysis teaches us nothing spatial or geographical about the psychic processes, but it certainly points to the temporal dimension. This dimension is all the more important if we can generalize the dialectics between "actual" and "psychic" to other major chapters of the Freudian theoretical construction.

At the *clinical* level, a temporal take on the workings of the psyche sheds new light on the decisive role of transference in psychoanalytic practice. It has important direct and indirect consequences for the handling of transference and more generally for the ethics of the analytic endeavor. Transference and, by the same token, countertransference can be seen as the central operator involved in the

---

[2] I think here, for instance of the present push, among North-American psychoanalysts for replacing repression with dissociation.

passage from what is actual (the repressed) to what is time-bound and linked to the complex time structure of personal history. In the present book, for example, I will refer more than once to the difference between two kinds of transference, depending on whether what is transferred stems from ready-made repressed *psychic* formations or from the *actual* nuclei of the unconscious. I shall contend that this difference is of major import regarding the practical and ethical disposition required of the analyst.

*

Obviously, the ideas expounded in this book were not elaborated in a void but resulted from a methodical reading of Freud. Both the method and the ideas were inherited, sometimes explicitly, other times implicitly, from the major thinkers and critical readers of Freud whose names will be mentioned throughout the book. Among them, Jean Laplanche stands out as a major influence, but I have also found inspiration in the works of non-analysts such as Lyotard— who was, among other things, a brilliant commentator of Freud— and Levinas, who did not overtly write about psychoanalysis but whose thinking strongly resonates with its ethics.

My wish is that the work presented here may incite and help the reader to take a new look at the Freudian heritage. While nothing of that heritage is thrown overboard here, the intention is to offer a different and possibly new itinerary through the vast landscape that was drawn by Freud, eventually finding new connections and transverse paths between some of the many roads that he has paved for us.

Dominique Scarfone
October 2015

A Matter of Time:
Actual Time and the Production of the Past*

In psychoanalytic theory, space metaphors are frequently used to describe the psychic apparatus. As for time, it is traditionally invoked under the heading of timelessness *of the* unconscious, *more aptly described as the resistance of the repressed to wearing away with time. This paper examines how the insertion of time into psychic events and structural differentiation form a single process. After looking into the parallelism between phenomenological and psychoanalytic views of time and differentiation, the author draws a distinction between two time categories:* chronological *versus* actual*. A clinical example is presented.*

> Drops of living past are what must be carefully preserved everywhere...as there are not too many on the whole planet...We possess no other life, no other sap than the treasures inherited from the past and digested, assimilated, recreated by us. Of all the human soul's needs, none is more vital than the past.
> —Simone Weil (1943)[1]

> The past is indestructible; sooner or later all things come back, and one of the things coming back is the project of abolishing the past.
> —Jorge Luis Borges (1993)

> To be conscious is to have time.
> —Emmanuel Lévinas (1971)

---

[1] This quotation and the two quotations immediately following were translated by the author.

*Originally published in 2006 in *Psychoanal. Q.*, 75: 807–834

This paper is about the work of psychoanalysis and how it is related to *being*, *having*, and *time*. *Being* will be addressed here in terms of the most fundamental stratum of psychic life, not directly accessible, as it belongs to a rather mythical state of narcissistic completeness. *Having*, as we shall see, will emerge when some differentiation has occurred within the state of being, with *loss* playing a decisive role. As for *time*, it is a multilayered concept that I will try in this paper to integrate more operationally into the workings of the psyche. More generally, I will try to show that these dimensions of experience are in fact bound together as parts of a global process of differentiation.

The work of psychoanalysis, as we know, can be described from many standpoints. Freud gave various versions of the ends and mechanisms of analysis: making the unconscious conscious, guessing (*erraten*) what is repressed and communicating it to the patient, lifting resistances, making ego be where id was, and so on. These were inserted into a model of the psychic apparatus based on an essentially spatial metaphor, yielding an easy-to-grasp, visual representation of the psyche. Freud nevertheless often referred to the time dimension of psychic events, namely by asserting the timelessness of unconscious processes. Time, however, did not benefit from an equal amount of attention on his part, so that quite late in his life, he would observe:

> Again and again I have had the impression that we have made too little theoretical use of this fact, established beyond any doubt, of the inalterability by time of the repressed. This seems to offer an approach to the most profound discoveries.[2]

I will suggest that if we pay sufficient attention to the time dimension in the workings of psychoanalysis, we may conclude that one of its most important goals is the production of the past. This may seem a bit surprising: isn't the psychoanalytic patient generally

---

2 Freud (1933 [1932]).

deemed a prisoner of the past? Isn't the past what analysis is supposed to deliver the patient from, so that he or she may enjoy the present and resume progression toward the future? The answer is yes, provided we are aware of how everyday psychoanalytic talk fails to consider the nature and status of what we spontaneously refer to as "the past." We may, of course, conveniently keep calling it "the past," but it is actually "the repressed," and one characteristic of the repressed is to return, to repeat itself, at least until a transformation occurs that turns it into history.

Philosophers have, by tradition, paid more attention to time than have scholars in any other discipline. I will therefore borrow mainly from two of them, Maurice Merleau-Ponty and Jean-François Lyotard. But the reader is asked to accept these borrowings at face value, as the purpose of this paper is not philosophical. I will in fact use but a few remarks from these authors, inasmuch as they seem to me to resonate usefully with—and help us shed some new light on—Freudian metapsychology.

Space and Time

It is not easy, perhaps impossible, to speak of time without reference to space or other physical metaphors[3]. Our experience is so deeply rooted in three-dimensional space, and movement within that space is so important for the experience of our bodily selves and the world around us, that we are naturally bent toward speaking of time itself with a spatial vocabulary. My purpose is therefore not to establish a purified notion of time, but rather to seriously consider Freud's assertion that unconscious processes are timeless, and see where this may take us regarding our understanding of the psyche.

Could this approach, for instance, spare us the problems we face by relying on our strictly space-laden metaphors of the mind?

---

3 Lakoff and Johnson (1999).

Convenient as they are, space metaphors are after all just metaphors, and problems arise when we try to go beyond the mere topography of "mental space" in our effort to describe the dynamic processes occurring therein. To give but one example, think of the structural model, in which Freud's final visual (i.e., spatial) representation of the psychic apparatus as a vesicle of living matter—with perception and the ego at the surface, the repressed and the drives deep inside[4]—is not a model that can actually be put to work. It is a static figure, clearly based on a schematic model of the human body. Now, while the body is the ultimate container of all our living processes, including those we approach from a psychological standpoint, what matters to us most is not the static body of anatomy, nor, for that matter, the objectified body of physiology, but rather the living body, the corporeal existence of a human being carrying on with its life. Space contains living and inert bodies alike, but only the living human—hence, the living psyche—is subjectively concerned with time.[5]

Following Ockham's principle of conceptual parsimony, I will try to leave aside the spatial metaphor (confident as I am that it will not disappear) and explore the possibility that the temporal dimension is sufficient for the description of the workings of the psyche in psychoanalytic terms. In so doing, I will be referring not to the time of physics, but to the specific dimension faced by human beings capable of reflective consciousness, as this entails the potential awareness of our finitude through the "passage of time." Consciousness is inseparable from existential time and chronology. To be sure, consciousness somehow espouses the "time arrow" of cosmology in the form of the irreversibility of individual and collective history; this, however, is

---

4 Freud (1924).
5 Freud's first model of the psyche of course constitutes another example of a space metaphor, with the theory of the double inscription after the lifting of repression. Freud (1915c) ponders whether, when repression is lifted, the de-repressed representation "moves" from the unconscious to the preconscious, or if it merely undergoes a functional change.

achieved at the cost of making the past a closed chapter within the trajectory of one's life history. As we know, the experience of analysis teaches us that reality is otherwise, and this has a huge impact on how we approach the functioning psyche.

It would appear that if consciousness is strongly correlated with the experience of time, Freud's idea of a timeless unconscious is a mere logical consequence of unconsciousness itself. But for the inventor of psychoanalysis, this concept was primarily the result of clinical observation. The description of memories emerging during treatment "with astonishing freshness"—that is, as if time had not in the least affected them—occurs as early as 1895, in the *Studies on Hysteria*[6], and remains a constant in Freud's conception of the mind until the very end. It must be noted, however, that while in the beginning Freud's conception may have pointed at the return of well-formed repressed memories, we know, from his paper on screen memories and other sources, that he did not think of memories as stable recordings popping up from some repository "in" the unconscious. We therefore adhere more specifically to the Freudian theory that memories are actively constructed in the present time out of repressed material, through forms that lend themselves to conveying something of the repressed, even though the latter—i.e., the truly timeless substratum—is not directly accessible[7]. The process is actually quite similar to how the manifest dream borrows figurative material from day residues to reflect repressed motions of desire.

We have numerous ways of verifying the clinical validity of Freud's take on the odd relationship between unconscious processes and chronological time. Think of the repetition compulsion, in which redundant patterns keep coming back as if no learning from experience occurred or no usable trace was left to mark the time of their return. Another example is the eruption of, as it were, "untimely"

---

6 Freud and Breuer (1895).
7 Freud (1985a), Freud (1915c).

mental contents in the otherwise normal flow of consciousness, where material that should belong to another time emerges in the present context as a foreign body. A third example is the fear of breakdown described by Winnicott, in which something seems to be threatening to happen in the future, whereas it has already happened in the past, but there was no ego to register it. Says Winnicott: "The original experience of primitive agony cannot be put in the past tense."[8]

Dreaming—and, as we shall see, parapraxes—provide other instances where the unpast (as I would call it) steps in. Confronted with phenomena such as these, psychoanalysis may be said to work toward their capture in a time net, or, if one prefers, toward the insertion of ordinary time into their midst.

Time and Differentiation

Psychoanalysis rests primarily on the spoken word. Access to unconscious processes and the transformation of timeless unconscious elements into conscious experience—and therefore into time-laden historicity—are fostered through speech. So we have before us the task of seeing what, if anything, links the spoken word to the insertion of time within psychic processes. In so doing, we shall see that the link between speech and time helps accomplish a general goal of psychoanalysis, that of achieving psychic differentiation. Let me first present a quasi-clinical example, a scene I had the opportunity to observe from up close, although outside of my professional endeavor, while waiting in line at the bank (this was before the widespread presence of ATMs).

> A woman stands near the counter waiting for a client to leave so that she may swiftly go up to the teller before the next client. This is perhaps the seventh time I have seen her repeating the maneuver, to the great dismay

---

8 Winnicott (1989 [1964]).

of the young teller behind the counter, who knows all too well what the woman is going to ask once again. Eyes to the ceiling, yet with a remnant of courteous manners, the teller once again reassures the woman that, yes, her savings are still there, and she prints one more statement to prove it. The woman thanks her dimly but will not leave the scene, merely stepping aside. No doubt about it: she's already doubting and will need yet another proof that between the time of the last printed statement and the present, no catastrophe has occurred—that there has not been some confusion in the bank's electronic circuits, erasing her account. We are clearly prepared for another round.

A cataclysm has probably occurred—but in the woman's mind. Some powerful unbinding process permits not even a 10-minute stability of her investment in her psyche.[9] A destructive motion has seemed to annihilate even the slightest confidence interval—as statisticians would say—in her inner world. Certainly, no one could have provided her with any final guarantee that her savings were perfectly safe. Nevertheless, among the people waiting in line at the bank that day, no one would have found her conduct reasonable, and she herself probably knew how excessive was her need to repeatedly verify her account.

The memory of this scene came back to me while reading a passage in the Phenomenology of Perception, where Merleau-Ponty writes that:

> If the past were available to us only in the form of express recollections, we should be tempted to continually recall it in order to verify their existence, just

---

9 *Investment* is a word that could easily—and in my view, advantageously—replace Strachey's pseudoscientific translation of *Besetzung* with *cathexis*. The strong homology of libidinal cathexis with financial investment would be thereby highlighted.

as this patient mentioned by Scheler, who had to constantly turn round to make sure that things were still there—whereas we feel they are behind us as an indisputable evidence.[10]

The problem of the woman in the bank could be understood as one of a continuous attack on the synthesis of time. Indeed, her paralyzing uncertainty could be conceived of more fundamentally as an uncertainty about the persistence of her own *being throughout time*. For her, time is not the continuous flow, the carrier wave upon which physical or mental events usually seem to occur; it looks rather like a succession of violent ridges eroding the very feeling of continuity. Every new moment represents a destruction of the past one, so that the familiar, seamless integration we normally experience, as the many stories of each of our days seem to merge into the single and stable stream we call our past, just does not seem to happen in her mind.

Interestingly enough, the synthesis of time can in turn be described in terms of differentiation. According to Merleau-Ponty, we should not think of time as a sequence. Rather, he suggests that "when time starts moving, it moves throughout its whole length. The 'instants' A, B, and C are not successively in being, but differentiate themselves from each other."[11] He states: "Since, in time, to be and to pass are synonyms, an event does not cease being when it becomes past…Time preserves what it has put into being at the very moment it expels it from being."[12] Merleau-Ponty seems to be saying that, contrary to what we are naturally brought to think, given our space-oriented conception of the psyche, the past is not the passive container of things bygone. The past, indeed, is our very being, and it can stay alive and evolve; the present is the passage where the retranscription and recontextualization of our past continually occur, in line

---

10 Merleau-Ponty (1945), p. 479. Translation by the author.
11 Merleau-Ponty (2012 [1945]), p. 487.
12 Op. cit., p. 480.

with Freud's[13] concept of Nachträglichkeit[14] (or deferred action, in Strachey's translation).

In terms of differentiation, one may also consider the woman's fear that her savings have vanished as a result of her inability to differentiate herself from her possessions, that is, to distinguish between *having* and *being*. Indeed, her anxiety over the possible loss of her savings was too pervasive to be attributed to an ordinary sense of risk. It rather looked as if her possessions were not in the domain of *having*, but instead were a part of her very *being*. One could also say that, by clinging to her possessions with the anguish of potentially losing them as soon as she turns her back, she is expressing the romantic idea that the passage of time can only mean destruction. She therefore needs to constantly check the persistence of her material possessions, as if to refute the destructive effect she attributes to time. In this way, she seems locked in a permanent *now*, which, as we shall see, is the trademark of the unconscious as we come to know it—for instance, through the repetition compulsion.

Hence, one may surmise that rejection of the flow of time, or rather of *her own passing through time*, is what brings about this woman's paralyzing uncertainty. From this perspective, her fear concerning her possessions can be seen as the mirror image of a fundamental anguish regarding the effect of time on her life in general. It then turns out that her refusal of time—and ultimately of death—is a refusal of *being*, since, as Merleau-Ponty remarks, to *be* is to *pass*. So she is locked in a paradox: by refusing time and loss, she is both wasting her time (and that of others, as we saw) and severely crippling her very being.

Contrary to the romantic view, destruction in the psyche is not the effect of time passing. At first glance, this may seem to contradict Freud's early view—when he thought that the repressed had to be brought to consciousness so that its ideational content could

---

13 Freud (1895a).
14 See, among others, Modell (1990); Laplanche (1992).

"wear away"[15]—but this is not the case, as the wearing away is not the equivalent of destruction. On the contrary, by becoming conscious, thoughts are subjected to judgment and compounded with other thoughts, thereby actually *generating* new thinking. Subjecting mental contents to time is therefore better conceived of as fostering transformation. What may look like destruction in this process is actually the conservation of something in a new form.[16]

As for real and damaging destruction, it rather takes the form of the repetition compulsion, as is suggested by Borges' aphorism quoted at the beginning of this article. This malignant form of circularity was, as we know, ascribed by Freud[17] to the "unbinding" effect of destructive forces in the psyche, subsumed under the idea of a death drive. The repetition compulsion, however, is not a direct expression of unbinding; it rather keeps the processes of the binding and unbinding of psychic elements locked within a demonic, unproductive duel. Since repetition may seem to go on forever, a tie (!) between the two processes is the apparent result. But there really is no tie.

The psyche may also be crippled by too much binding, as modern history has shown with the collectively submissive psychology of the masses united and entranced under the erotic spell of some charismatic leader.[18] In repetition, unbinding is the real winner, as time, and therefore being, is held captive to a circular motion, resisting transformation and allowing for little novelty or creativity. This probably has something to do with Freud's persistent contention that timelessness is a hallmark of the repressed unconscious.

From Being to Having

For Jean-François Lyotard, phenomenological time, i.e., time

---

15 Freud and Breuer (1895).
16 The Hegelian concept of *Aufhebung*—at once transcending and preserving—applies here.
17 Freud (1920) and Freud (1924).
18 Zaltzman (1997).

as we experience it, is inscribed in the structure of articulate phrases. For instance, time is introduced with the use of personal pronouns, within an I-Thou polarity, where no two proper names can occupy the same pronominal pole simultaneously. I and Thou are deictic, i.e., they define two positions in the dialogue.[19] For a dialogue to take place, the proper names that occupy these pronominal places must necessarily alternate. Writes Lyotard (1991):

> To this possibility of permutation immediately corresponds the sequence of two phrases, a temporality. When addressing "Thou," "I" expects the coming of a phrase in which the two names will have traded their places on the poles of destination. Such disposition is the kernel of temporality in the phenomenological sense.[20]

Notice that in Lyotard's description, the constitution of time also entails a differentiation similar to the one posited by Merleau-Ponty (1945) in the passage quoted earlier. However, Lyotard is not considering time in itself; he rather underscores the differentiation as indicated and steadily confirmed by the alternating positions of the proper names on I-Thou poles of conversation. The phenomenological sense of time emerges because Ms. A and Mr. B must continually trade their positions of speaker and listener if they are to really talk to each other. A phrase can only follow another phrase.

Think now of one of Freud's posthumously published aphorisms:

> [Regarding]…"having" and "being" in children. Children like expressing an object-relation by an iden-

---

19 *Deictic* is defined as "having the function of pointing out or specifying, and having its reference determined by the context (the words 'this,' 'there,' and 'you' are *deictic*)" (Webster's New World College Dictionary).
20 Lyotard, "Voix" (1991a), p. 135. Translation by the author.

tification: "I am the object." "Having" is the later of the two, after loss of the object it relapses into "being." Example: the breast. "The breast is a part of me, I am the breast." Only later: "I have it"—that is, "I am not it."[21]

What happens if we bring together Freud's imaginary scene and Lyotard's dipole? We are at first struck by one major difference: in the scene painted by Freud, the trading of places on the I-Thou dipole is not yet realized. On the one hand, there is simply no I and no *Thou* at this stage. Nothing may reply to "I am the breast"; this is not even an articulate phrase to begin with, but rather a virtual sentence simply inferred by Freud. Lacking the *I* and the *Thou*, the phrase cannot yield the alternating positions. There being no deictic, time cannot yet emerge. For there to be a reply—a phrase to come—and therefore for the existence of alternating I-Thou positions, a previous differentiation is needed. In Freud's virtual scene, this means passing from *being* to *having*.

Writes Freud: "Only later: 'I have it'—that is, 'I am not it.'" Trying to think this transformation through, we soon find that it cannot follow a simple sequence. We do not evolve from *I am* to *I have* by way of a linear development. Reaching the stage of "I have it—that is, I am not it" represents a major step, supported by many implicit mental operations relating to the central notion of *loss*. Hence, we must now examine how this notion is born.

Normally, loss is about something that we have. Therefore, since we are, on the contrary, suggesting that *to have* is what emerges from the notion of *loss*, we are forced to think of a loss occurring even before *having* is realized. Losing before having—is this even conceivable? Before we try answering this question, we may notice that "I am the breast," even as a virtual phrase that no infant ever uttered as such, is still much too articulate. Indeed, the verb to be as conjugated in this phrase is not playing its usual role as a copula. A copula is meant to unite two *different* things—the subject and its predicate—

---

21 Freud (1938).

whereas this Freudian sentence indicates that there is no difference between *I* and *breast*.

In "I am the breast," therefore, the breast is not the predicate, and *I* is only a grammatical subject—that is, it refers to the subject of the enunciated sentence, but not to the subject of enunciation—and quite understandably so, since in the situation described by Freud, there is no enunciation proper. To understand this better, we shall take into account an essential difference introduced by Lyotard between two different kinds of phrases: the *articulate phrase* and the *phrase of affect*.

The expression *phrase of affect* may look like an oxymoron, as it evokes precisely something that cannot be made into phrases. In the hope of avoiding serious misunderstandings, we need to make our terms more explicit. First, we must keep in mind that the term *affect*—which is often used as a synonym for *feeling* or *emotion*—has a more restrictive meaning in the present context. Here it refers to what Freud mentioned as the "quantitative factor," sometimes specified as an "amount of affect" (*Affektbetrag*).[22] Thus, *affect* is a name for a psychic representative that refers to some raw material in need of being psychically elaborated; it is not the nonverbal equivalent of something that could as well be conveyed by words. Therefore, the term *phrase of affect* evokes a phrase that is not uttered, and about which another (articulate) phrase has yet to be created. Nevertheless, in Lyotard's conception, referring to a *phrase* is justified by the fact that language is always summoning us, and that the unit of language that we usually deal with is not the phoneme, but the phrase. To sum up, in Lyotard's own words, "human beings discover…that they are summoned by language…to recognize that what remains to be phrased exceeds what they can presently phrase, and that they must be allowed to institute idioms which do not yet exist."[23] This, I believe, speaks directly to the work of psychoanalysis.

---

22 Freud (1915b).
23 Lyotard (1988), p. 13

Going back to the I-Thou dipole, we must consider that articulating a phrase—and waiting for another phrase to come back in reply—does not imply that the second phrase is of a similar nature to the first one. The oncoming phrase may be a phrase of affect, which Lyotard describes as entertaining a *differend*—a radical dissension—with the articulate phrase. The latter is not symmetrical to the former. A phrase of affect is a phrase that "overloads the body-thought, the psychic apparatus," and such overload makes for "the presence of a phrase that does not signify (is it pleasure or pain?), is not addressed (from whom, to whom?) and has no reference (what is it about?), a phrase that arrives impromptu in the course of phrases."[24] As we shall see, another important aspect of the phrase of affect is that its temporality is not differentiated, as it always exists in the now—a now that must not be mistaken for the present tense. Writes Lyotard: "I insist: the now of affect is not surrounded by a *before* and an *after*."[25]

If the verb *to be* in "I am the breast" is not a copula, if it denotes not a subject and a predicate but the total identity of *I* and *breast*, then we may conclude that, in spite of appearances to the contrary, the whole situation belongs to the category of *phrases of affect*. Indeed, were it able to *articulate* such a phrase, the infant would not be an infant any more (remember that in Latin, infans literally means "one who cannot speak"). By possessing some ability to speak, the infant would also have already distinguished between *I* and *breast*, positing them as separate elements to be reunited by the verb *am*—now a true copula—and, more generally, by the use of words that represent things. Hence, the scene belongs to the domain of phrases of affect.

The change required in order to bring the infant from "I am the breast" to "I have it—that is, I am not it," must be a change concerning affect. We must therefore ask ourselves what the possible affective

---

24 Lyotard "Emma," (2002 [2000]), p. 75. Translation by the author.
25 Lyotard "Voix," (1991a), p. 136. Translation by the author.

meaning of such a change is. For this, we will first describe the logical aspect of the change and then consider how it can actually occur.

The Logic of Loss

Going from *I am* to *I have* constitutes a shattering of the totality implied by the full (though obviously imaginary) identity of *I* and *breast*. This breach in imaginary completeness can be thought of as a *loss of being*. And since there is yet no phenomenal time involved, we are also compelled to think that, from a temporal standpoint, this loss is felt as if it had always already occurred. In other words, a *loss of being* can only be conceived of *retrospectively* as the loss of the illusory sense of continuity, from the standpoint of someone who no longer feels such continuity. Noticeably, with the expression *loss of being*, we are reminded of Lacan's *lack of being*,[26] or, in reverse, of Winnicott's *going on being*[27]—the basic tendency in the infant upon which the environment will inevitably impinge.

The important thing here is the *sense of loss*, i.e., the *affective* sense that something has changed, that a *difference* has been introduced. Loss indeed leads to the sense and the importance of having. Only from sensing a difference can the psyche begin distinguishing between the thing itself and its predicates. Interestingly, this was described by Freud as early as 1895 in the Project for a Scientific Psychology, where he discussed the function of thought and judgment.[28] The effective source of such difference remains, however, to be found, and we will look for it further on in this paper.

For now, if we go back to the scene imagined by Freud in 1938, we posit that from the sense that a difference has been introduced, a change ensues in which the breast is now truly a predicate, an attribute, instead of being engulfed in a complete identity. This is most

---

26 Lacan (1966).
27 Winnicott (1964).
28 Freud (1895a).

important for the logic of our argument, since an attribute is something that can be lost. So, whereas a *loss of being* points toward the loss of some ideal, narcissistic totality (one that in reality is nowhere to be found), we must nevertheless consider the transformation it implies as a real event that we will later try to describe. Thus, except in psychotic thinking or in playful, imaginative thinking, "I am the breast" ends up being a contradictory phrase that must be left behind in order to make room for another phrase, such as "I have it."

Reaching this conclusion marks the simultaneous birth of the feelings of *having* and *not having*. These are born together, since one can never experience the feeling of *having* by itself. To have something is, implicitly, to know that one may not always have it, or that one might not have had it in the first place. Were it not for such negation, indeed, one would not even notice one's possessions (affirmation), and hence one would relapse into *being*. The relationship between *to have* and *to lose*, therefore, has a staunch solidarity.

We are thus reminded of the woman at the bank: her doubts regarding the continuity of *having* reflected her problem in accepting that *to have* always entails the risk of losing—or, better, that loss is the intrinsic trait of every possession. By refusing the inherent loss, the woman "fell back on being," as Freud would have it—that is, she identified with her possessions, struggling against the primeval loss that at some point has marked us all.

The Realization of Loss and the Birth of Time

By bringing together the virtual infant-breast scene proposed by Freud and the I-Thou dipole, and discussing their logic, we have not yet introduced temporality. We have not examined how the situation actually evolves. After having explored in the preceding section the logic of the progression from *being* to *having*, we must now try to appreciate how this transformation can actually occur. We saw that such progression requires the infant to take notice of some *difference* emerging and shattering the "going on being."[29] *Difference* is therefore another word for *loss of being*.

Difference can be ascribed to many factors, but in my view it is most usefully attributed to the impact, the impingement of the Other. This may sound like a truism ("Otherness installs difference—big deal!"), so we must discuss it in further detail.

In the Freudian scene we have been discussing, Otherness steps in because the breast in question is not simply the adequate object of the infant's need, the "pacifier" of its inner tension. As Laplanche[30] pointed out, it is ironic that even within the field of psychoanalysis, one must be reminded that the breast is a significant part of the woman's (the mother's) sexual endowment. The breast, even from within the nurturing relationship with the baby, signifies a fact of seduction. Even in the most normal situation, it plays an excitatory role. This fact was already acknowledged by Freud when, after he revoked his seduction theory, he nevertheless spoke of the mother as an "involuntary seductress."[31]

Laplanche[32] inserts this idea in a renewed, more encompassing theory of generalized seduction. In Laplanche's model, the infant is necessarily exposed to messages emanating from the world of adult caretakers—messages contaminated by the adult's own repressed sexual contents. These messages are seductive in that they "divert" (this is the primary meaning of the Latin seducere) the innate channels of communication between adult and child, attracting the child's attention toward their enigma, initiating an unending process of investigation, translation, and theorizing.[33] The seductive "breast" is therefore a metonymy for the seductive situation as a whole, for

---

29 Winnicot (1964).
30 Laplanche (1989 [1987]).
31 Freud (1905b); see also Freud (1938).
32 Laplanche (1989 [1987]).
33 From a totally different perspective, the idea of "child as theorist" has also been put forward by cognitive psychologists Gopnik and Meltzoff (1997).

which Laplanche coined the expression fundamental anthropological situation. According to this view, Winnicott's impingement, then, does not occur due to the environment's failures alone; rather, it results primarily from the mother's (the adult's) excitatory action, even while she is satisfying the infant's vital needs and tending to the baby's continuity of being.[34]

To be able to take difference into account, the infant will need to process the impact of the stimulating other. Staying with Freud's example of the breast, we will now consider that its excitatory role is what causes it to take a place in the oncoming I-Thou dipole. The excitatory breast formulates, so to speak, a first phrase of its own, a phrase that creates some disturbance, what might be called "noise" in the channels of communication ("normal" communication being that of the mother's response in feeding the infant or just appeasing it with the nipple). So, whereas a dipole is here being sketched out, it is not yet effective, since the two phrases—the infant's "I am the breast," and the breast's *excitatory phrase*—do not yet come together, and therefore do not put the alternating deictic positions into motion. No time is generated from this as a result, but instead, two timeless postures come into being: that of the infant with "I am the breast," and that of the breast with its excitatory message.

Time then steps in when the infant notices that there is a message from the other (despite its enigmatic nature) and tries to make sense of it, to translate it. Indeed, translating means differentiating the bulk of the message into a part that can be assimilated—literally, *made similar* to or compatible with the ego—and a part that, given the infant's incapacity to fully master the excitatory aspect, remains incompatible, intractable. Resisting translation, that part of the message can be said to be *repressed* (primal repression). As Freud wrote: "A failure of

---

[34] Gantheret (1998), and Pontalis (1997b) have expressed a similar criticism of Winnicott's view, but Laplanche (1989 [1987]) is the one who expounded the theoretical framework that extends beyond the relation to the breast, in his theory of generalized seduction.

translation—this is what is known clinically as 'repression.'"[35] Thus, difference is imposed upon the infant not because of abstract otherness, but by way of the excitatory character of the message emanating from the Other (in this instance, the breast, but this is only one possible form).

Taking notice of the enigmatic message (by working at translating it) amounts to sensing the introduction of some difference, i.e., perceiving the breach in the continuity of being and realizing a loss of being. One way of seeing this is that loss already haunts the object, so to speak, even before it is conceived of as an object—that is, even prior to differentiation.[36] It is the Other's own unconscious that makes for the sheer otherness of its message and constitutes the actual loss.[37]

The occurrence of the passage from being to having, the foundational moment of differentiation, means that the infant is somewhat compelled to "acknowledge reception" of the message of the Other.[38] Acknowledging reception means sensing the disturbance that impinges on the apparent "going on being."[39] By accounting for what was received—that is, by processing it, partially translating it—the infant is also sensing a delay: the time it needs for grasping a first meaning and repudiating what cannot be grasped (what, in Freud's words, "evades being judged."[40]) For the infant, this is an unfinished business, since for all the translation achieved, the mystery of the excitatory message still lingers and more work will be required.

This, then, is how time enters the scene: through the work of translation.

We can now see how the *I-Thou* dipole and the Infant–Breast duality coincide. The sequence goes like this:

---

35 Freud (1985), p. 208
36 Scarfone (2003).
37 This is not unlike Lacan's lack in the Other (1966).
38 Scarfone (2003).
39 Winnicott (1989 [1964]).
40 Freud (1895a).

1. Two phrases of affect are issued, at first without interacting:

A. The breast's (the object's, the Other's) phrase is an excitatory phrase of affect;

B. The infant's primal phrase of affect is that of complete identification: "I am the breast."

Both are *virtual phrases*, and language is not part of the scene.

2. Sooner or later, the infant will have to acknowledge reception of the excitatory message of the Other, even if its processing is deferred. Thereafter (so to speak):

C. The infant partially translates the message, differentiating between the parts that are compatible and those incompatible with the emerging ego. The parts compatible fall in the domain of the predicate, i.e., *to have*; they can therefore be lost. This means that:

D. The object can now become absent and can be acknowledged as such.

Translation (C, above) and the *message of absence* (D) will eventually lead toward the ability to create more articulate phrases. When this is achieved, the deictic dipole and temporality can begin to operate concurrently with the advent of language. What we see, then, is that *time is introduced along with primal repression*, as the latter separates what is compatible from what is incompatible, untranslatable. The birth of time, therefore, occurs in parallel with the structural differentiation of the psyche.[41]

It must be stressed that, whereas translation is a primal structuring fact, it nevertheless operates in the psyche all the time. It is, at any given moment, a matter of articulating—however incompletely—an unarticulated phrase. In Lyotard's view, it is the task of

---

[41] Hence, psychic conflict is also entering the scene at this point.

taking into account something in excess of *lexis* or *logos*, i.e., in excess of enunciation, something that presents itself as the *phônè*—the Greek term for the voice and its timbre or tone. In Freudian terms, *lexis* and *phônè* could be linked with the drives, in that *lexis* amounts to representation, while *phônè* is related to affect (representation and affect being the psychic representatives of the drives).

The *fort/da* example reported by Freud[42] is a good illustration of the emergence of such symbolic function. When the mother leaves, she emits, so to speak, an *excitatory message* related to her going away. The baby is not only frustrated by losing sight of the mother, but also provoked into doing something about it (translating it), both through gesture and rudimentary speech. The baby begins by repeating the experience of loss, and only later is he or she able to symbolize the mother's departure *and* return. The baby can now "have" the mother at will. But loss came first.

Actual Time and the Present Tense

We have seen that, according to Lyotard, time emerges from the permutation that occurs on the pronominal ends of a dialogue, i.e., from there being two consecutive phrases. We have then examined what would be required for this to apply to the infant-breast situation. Regarding time, we used the verb *emerge*, since we posited that, for the infant, phenomenological time does not yet exist, since the two *phrases* that occurred in that situation could only be inarticulate phrases of affect. These phrases reflected two timeless postures that did not interact as in an I-Thou dialogue; therefore, phenomenal or chronological time did not operate. This is not surprising, as the time of a phrase of affect—the time of *phônè*—is always now. Indeed, as long as it remains disconnected from the articulate phrase, affect has no history. In such a case, its eruption is always an actual experi-

---

42 Freud (1920).

ence, a *presentation* rather than a *re-presentation*.

But here an objection arises: does time really emerge? Doesn't producing chronological time out of the *now* of affect rather amount to extracting time from time itself? Isn't time already embedded in the word *now*? Even more importantly, doesn't this way of thinking challenge the very idea of timeless unconscious processes?

Indeed, we seem to be extracting time from time itself, if only because ordinary language necessarily implies a temporal connotation, and we always speak from a time-laden standpoint. On the other hand, when Freud speaks of a timeless unconscious, he means that time does not seem to pass or to affect unconscious thought processes. Pontalis[43] also insists on this way of viewing unconscious time. But we have seen that time does not pass from Merleau-Ponty's phenomenological standpoint as well. So how can timelessness remain a distinctive feature of unconscious processes, if conscious (phenomenal) time itself does not pass?

There is a way out of this apparent impasse, and it is already implicit in Freud's thinking. To begin with, we have insisted, with Lyotard,[44] that the *now* of a phrase of affect is not the *present tense* (if this were the case, it would entail the past and the future, the two other instances of ordinary existential time). As for the meaning of this *now*, we will make it a bit clearer by calling it *actual time*.[45] Actual time is a preferable term here since it not only means now, but also implies the dimension of the *act* (Freud's *Agieren*). It signals a time that is concrete and effective and not merely a measured time span. This is congruent with the fact that the phrase of affect is itself an act affecting, as it were, our being. Inasmuch as it is not yet articulate, i.e.,

---

43 Pontalis (1997b)
44 Lyotard (1988); (1991a); (2002 [2000]).
45 In French psychoanalysis, the term actuel is derived from Freud's terms *Aktuell* and *Aktual*, as in *Aktualneurosen*, the actual neuroses. I am well aware that in English, the word *actual* is already loaded with other familiar meanings, but there seems to be no better translation available for these German terms.

not yet translated into the second kind of phrase, a phrase of affect is impervious to chronological time and therefore prone to repetition.

We should here refer back to the ever-fresh reminiscences of the *Studies on Hysteria*,[46] but also, and more importantly, to the "actual neuroses"—anxiety neurosis and neurasthenia—that Freud considered to be lurking in the background of unconscious fantasy and therefore not amenable to analysis.[47] In our present vocabulary, we shall say that, by contrast with the "psychoneuroses"—hysteria and obsessive neurosis—the actual neuroses lack the dimension of the articulate phrase. This explains their mainly affective (anxiety neurosis) or somatic (neurasthenia) presentation. But at one point, Freud suggested that in psychoneurosis, there is frequently a nucleus of actual neurosis.[48] This statement might reveal itself to be quite useful in solving the problem we have just encountered regarding the timelessness of the unconscious. What if, indeed, Freud's ideas of the timelessness of unconscious processes and the actual nucleus in every "psycho-neurosis" really refer to the same phenomenon?

We have seen that those processes that were not yet inscribed in a time sequence (past-present-future) tend to repeat themselves— that is, to occur in an ever-*present* form; they are presentations instead of re-presentations, *acts* (*Agieren*) instead of *thoughts*, or *phrases of affect* instead of *articulate phrases*. In this perspective, the psychoanalytic endeavor of articulating—translating, transforming—the phrase of affect is tantamount to working through actual time—the time of the act, the time of repetition—and transferring it, however incompletely, into psychic representation. Something amenable to articulation can and must be extracted from the ore of inarticulate phrases of affect. In other words, we work to transpose the now, the actual time of the unconscious, into the realm of chronological time.

---

46 Freud and Breuer (1895)
47 Freud (1898b) ; see also Freud (1915-17):389-ff.
48 Freud (1915-17):390.

A phrase of affect can engender time because the *actual* or the *now* quality of the inarticulate phrase is in itself a form of time, although by no means what we usually call by that name. Such *affecting time* or *concrete time*, although in need of being articulated, is nevertheless endowed with a *momentum*, a thrust. For Freud, just as affect was to be considered in terms of quantity, the drives were said to have a physical momentum. We saw that a phrase of affect, with its *now* form of time, is *presenting* (rather than *re*-presenting) a message to the receiver. (It is worth mentioning that, just like translation, this is not specific to the infant--adult situation, but occurs at any age.) When a well-differentiated psychic structure is already in place, such *presentation* of the inarticulate phrase of affect has two possible results: either what is presented is rejected, denied, repressed, or, to the contrary, its impact is acknowledged, somehow shaking the psychic structure and provoking anxiety. We shall shortly see how, provided the necessary containment is available, temporality will then swing over from *now* to the *present tense*, giving birth to chronological time.

This by no means implies that the process just described follows a single mode of action. In a general sense, this is what transference is all about: something *actual*, a *presentation* belonging to the realm of *Agieren*, the act—something that needs to be worked through toward *representations*. Sometimes words are found to name affect, while at other times it is affect that reaches some already-present but as yet "unaffected" representation. Another frequent occurrence in analysis is one in which affect presents itself *in person*, so to speak—as an inarticulate phrase, provoking a major interference, a functional aphasia in the subject, as we often witness with slips or parapraxes. The following clinical example will illustrate this.

Eine Kleine Kannibalische Musik[49]

A patient of mine, Florence, was one day trying to remember the name of a famous pianist, "*Claudio* something," whose playing she felt was so gentle. The only name she was able to come up with at first was *Claudio Abbau*, but this certainly was not it. She then thought of *Claudio Abbado*, only to discard him as a conductor. Finally, the correct name emerged: *Claudio Arrau*.

Now it happened that she had just dreamt of a dog, a Great Dane attacking and devouring two men. About one of the victims, Florence had thought in the dream: "Well done with him, so he won't play at being a psychoanalyst again!" No doubt, the affective charge is important in this dream but, as we shall see, this was not really a crude manifestation of affect. It turned out that the dream was the end product of a series of permutations regarding both affect and representations. The Great Dane, indeed, alluded to other meanings that Florence mentioned en passant, such as in the following comment: "Last week, I literally stuffed myself with nuts." In this sentence, I could not help hearing the French sound of *nuts* (*noix*)—this analysis being conducted in French—embedded in the *Dane* (*danois*), and I told the patient so.

My comment elicited a series of associations from the patient opening upon her oedipal story. Nuts and chocolate, indeed, happened to be the only foods that her mother had kept locked away from the children, in a kitchen drawer, reserving them primarily for her husband (Florence's father). This apparently trivial fact took on quite a significant meaning, as Florence later learned that these foods had become one of the meager means of seduction that her mother was still using toward her husband, whom she knew to be a womanizer. The nut reserve was to appear in retrospect as a way—however clumsy—of salvaging the remains of an oedipal triangle that had been seriously damaged by the father. He had indeed pushed his

---

49 Here I offer my apologies to Mozart!

womanizing close to incest when he started secretly dating a young lady who, as Florence would learn much later, was none other than her best friend. Thus, the store of nuts in reserve gave the mother some consistency, preventing her complete disappearance from the oedipal scene.

Looking in retrospect at this material, the oedipal structure appears to have been supported by a rudimentary primal scene in which the father's "nuts" were locked inside the mother's "drawer." More interesting to me, however, is the fact that Florence's search for the name of the pianist resulted from the impulse provided by the dream, as I shall now explain.

After listening to the series of surnames that came up as possibly being the pianist Claudio's, I did not know what to think of them, so I jotted them down in a column on a sheet of paper:

ABBAU

ABBADO

ARRAU

In looking at the column, I then felt that the three names could be superimposed, and wondered what would result if one erased all the letters that were common to the three words. So I barred the letters A, B, and U, which left a DO and an RR:

~~ABBAU~~

~~ABB~~ADO

ARR~~AU~~

I then mentioned this to Florence, while noting (at first only to myself) that DO was the first syllable of my first name, and that RR felt like the growl of some hungry/angry animal. When I added this last bit of information to what I had already told Florence, she was startled: the Great Dane of her dream had popped up, this time not as a representation, but as something *actual*—not a dream figure, but a vibrant, expressive form: a phrase of affect, or *phônè*. The voracious dog was not simply *evoked*; it was *there*, in the *phônè* carried over by her double slip from the actual time of her unconscious, presenting itself as a threatening growl just when Florence was searching for a pianist with a gentle touch.

In the following sessions, we were led, thanks to other dreams, to the anorexia of the patient's adolescence, as well as to the strange illness that broke out in her mouth after her mother committed suicide—a rare ailment that threatened her with the loss of all her teeth. These were stories she well knew—stories of repressed devouring and problematic introjections—but they were stories that, like the Great Dane of her dream, needed to be brought back to life *in the flesh*[50] in order to be articulated.

The devouring thrust that presented itself in the transference through the dream and within the parapraxes (where they were more deeply embedded, but even more effective) was not (or not yet) something evoking the past, nor was it at first really *present*. The thrust was *actual*, and as such it was a phrase of affect that *acted* on Florence's thought processes. Only through the classic compromise formation of her slip could this unconscious thrust become *represented* in the transference. Her effort at articulating her desire formed a word representation conveying the menacing growl while hiding it from view. The analysis—the dislocation—of the slip would in turn bring us down to the level of *presentation* of the actual unconscious thing. Conflating the three words of Florence's consecutive slips was only possible and productive insofar as they belonged to another form of time. Their unconscious status yielded the final RR by allowing them to be superimposed— i.e., to be treated not as words with a spatially distributed sequence, but as the timeless vehicles of something that cannot really be put in writing: the growl of a hungry/angry beast.

---

50 Gantheret (1998).

My aim in presenting this vignette is not to introduce some purportedly new psychoanalytic technique—actually, it does not represent any customary procedure of my practice—but to illustrate a more general idea: the idea that parapraxes—or, for that matter, remembering and gaining insight in analysis—do not result from simple shifts between well-organized and meaningful representations. Rather, they are driven by what has been inarticulate, closer to *force* than to *meaning*—tending toward meaning, to be sure, but with no preexisting meaning that would lie there undercover, waiting to be found. Meaning is introduced *de novo*, along with time.

Concluding Remarks

In trying to make metapsychology reside only in the dimension of time, we have come to observe that the idea of timeless unconscious processes must be questioned. How could something human escape the grip of time? We have seen, however, that for Freud, timelessness meant at one point that repressed contents do not wear away. If we stick with this definition of timelessness, we see that the repressed *does* carry a form of temporality, but that it evades *chronological* time. In other words, the repressed is what lies outside the past-present-future categories in which thoughts and feelings wear away by combining with others of their kind and being worked through into newer thinking and affect.

If the unconscious must be said to bear some form of time, then it is in the *actual* form—a time without memory, since it is the time of the thing that is always acted now. It is also the time of the *phônè*, the time of manifestation, the time of the drives' momentum, and not yet the time of articulation. Actual time is the time of phrases of affect upon which it is the task of analysis to act so that they can be articulated, so that they can become part of the past and therefore give way to subjective differentiation.

As for Florence, a number of years passed before she was able to articulate the pain of loss and absence without being engulfed by it. Time, however, finally took hold of her story, making her more real, more free. In a letter written to me some months after the end of her analysis, she used the words *golden dust* to describe what she had gained from our work together: gold, the incorruptible, and dust, into which everything turns in the end. Florence obviously used these words without any reference to what I have just presented, but the two words form an apt metaphor, alluding to time as it does not pass, and also to us as we pass through time—hopefully knowing that our past is behind us and that we need not look back repeatedly to make sure it is still there.

Acknowledgments: The author wishes to thank Lewis Kirshner, M.D., and Dawn Skorczewski, Ph.D., for their help with a preliminary version of this paper.

Repetition:
Between Presence and Meaning*

The notion of "repetition" is explored from a metapsychological point of view in relation with the specific meaning of "remembering" in psychoanalysis and with other major dimensions of psychic life, such as binding, transference and time. Drawing from Freud and post-Freudian authors, the author revisits the analytic process, suggesting that whereas a preliminary stratum of analysis deals with meaning, the analytic method is eventually conducive beyond meaning, to presence.

Repetition usually implies comparison. Something is said to repeat itself whenever we can apprehend it from a reference point, a comparable thing of which it is the reiteration. In the psychoanalytic field, however, this is not exactly so. Freud's exploration of the relationships between remembering, repeating, and working-through introduces important features of human affairs that usually go unseen in too general a view of repetition. If we consider the operational definition of *remembering* (*Erinnern*) formulated in the 1914 paper as "reproduction in the psychical field,"[1] repetition itself takes a very specific meaning. Repetition is indeed the term for what Freud would

---

[1] Excerpt from Freud (1895a). When I quote from Freud I use the newer French translation of the *Complete Works* (*Oeuvres complètes de Freud: Psychanalyse*. Paris: PUF) and translate from the French. Their equivalents in the Standard Edition are in the References.

*First presented at the 45th Congress of the International Psychoanalytic Association, Berlin, 27 July 2007. The translation is by the author.

call *Agieren* ("action") as opposed to *Erinnern*.[2] If we also put in the equation the well-known toggle switch between thinking and action, it follows that whatever stands outside of psychic elaboration should be deemed a repetition. This has important consequences in both practice and theory. Under this definition, indeed, repetition yields a specific understanding of what is repeated in the transference, which in turn may influence our analytical conduct.

Regarding theory, one could say that when Freud turned his attention to repetition, he was already engaging, perhaps unknowingly, in what was to become his major theoretical turn in the 1920s. Among its many features, the incipient revolution in Freud's thinking involved delving always deeper into metapsychology, relying less on the sensual-empirical point of view and thinking ever more in terms of principles—fundamental principles that ended up including the drives as well. While the analytical encounter with a fellow human continued providing the clinical experience, the conceptualization of such experience was less and less a replica of what was observed. It ensues from Freud's metapsychological views of 1914 that a single *Agieren* is always already a repetition, for the simple reason that it rests outside the psychical field. This should not come as a surprise. Psychoanalysis, after all, is a discipline concerned with living systems and these are always highly redundant, tending towards reproducing themselves indefinitely. Freud's ideas about repetition are therefore not as much a discovery as the consistent result of the study of psychic life. He actually wrote that by highlighting the repetition compulsion he did not obtain any new fact, but rather "gained a more unified view."[3]

But to state that a single "act" (*Agieren*) is a repetition may seem a bit preposterous, so I will try to make the argument clear. We saw that, as opposed to remembering, repetition is whatever lies outside the psychical domain. We should not indeed lose sight of the fact

---

2 Freud (1914a)
3 Op. cit.

that Freud assigns to analysis the aim of "remembering." From the outset in his paper Freud mentioned that while, descriptively, *remembering* is "filling in the lacunæ of memory," from a dynamic standpoint it means "overcoming the resistance of repression." So if we now take into account what Freud put under the heading of *repression*—a concept he was elaborating in that same period[4]—then *remembering* in psychoanalysis cannot be the banal act of "recalling" or "evoking." It rather implies the transmutation of some material into a new form and a change in its economic status. We will get back to this later.

For now, let us notice that if remembering means "reproduction in the psychical field," it ensues that, as Loewald had clearly seen, remembering is itself a form of repetition.[5] We then have repetition at every level of the experience of psychoanalysis. Repetition, therefore, really *does* provide a unitary view of what goes on in the body-mind systems as they are summoned up by the analytic method. What we should ask then is *under what form* we encounter repetition. We obviously welcome repetition in the form of "remembering," because it is something that can be contained in the psychical domain and therefore undergo a number of psychic transformations through the thinking processes. *Contained* here means both "delimited" and, to some extent, "restrained" or "controlled." This by no means implies a complete mastery of psychical processes. It means, however, that some *delay* has been introduced where once there reigned a mechanism of automatic and immediate response. In other words, *language* and *time* have entered the scene heretofore dominated by repetition. And if in the *Agieren* language and time—two of the most significant features of consciousness—were absent, there was no real consciousness at work, even though there could be awareness of something taking place.

Here again we see what difference runs between a purely

---

4 Freud (1915b).
5 Loewald (2000 [1973]).

empirical take on repetition and the metapsychological conception. Thus, when acting (*Agieren*) occurs, it is by definition always too late for any form of control. The act has already been perpetrated and the conscious ego cannot but rationalize its occurrence. Hence, it matters little if the acting does not readily appear as a repetition in the empirical sense. It is repetition all the same in the metapsychological sense, inasmuch as the subject was not in the position of *deliberately* planning the event or of *speaking* (at least to himself or herself) with sufficient insight about its *meaning*. This is important, since if we require "sufficient insight" about the meaning of our actions, it ensues that there is always a *measure of repetition* in whatever we do or say. But not surprisingly so. What indeed is a person's character, or, at a larger level, what is a given culture if not a set of repetitive features? But if we are always repeating to a certain extent, it follows that, in turn, *remembering* takes on an even more specific meaning.

While repetition constitutes the basic level of mental functioning, remembering must be located at the apex of mental activity as a fragile, pulsating, discontinuous, almost evanescent feature. It consists in the momentary possession or repossession of one's thoughts and feelings. Remembering is recomposing one's whole mind. It is not just adding some new item to one's mental scrapbook, since such a scrapbook is nowhere to be found in the mind. Gaining some significant new memory is not simply adding to what was already there; it requires a complete reshuffling of one's psyche; it involves a specific temporal mechanism which Freud sometimes referred to as *Nachträglichkeit*, translated and widely used as après-coup in the French psychoanalytic tradition; a notion that Arnold Modell also recaptured to a certain extent with the concept of *recontextualization*.[6] The idea is also supported by contemporary neuroscience. Think, for instance, of Edelman's work on the "remembered present".[7] To be

---

6 Modell (1990).
7 Edelman (1989).

sure, *to remember* is etymologically different from *to dismember*, but one is tempted to bring the two together in opposition. This works in English as well as in French and in Italian, and even with the Spanish substantive *remembranza*, which appears to be the opposite of *desmembramiento*. But whereas from a purely linguistic point of view these words are unrelated, the antinomy between dismembering and remembering can be sustained if we think of remembering as a constant recomposing of the whole mindset, as a restoration, while repetition in action can be seen as reflecting disorganization. Interestingly enough, a similar idea is mentioned in the *Confessions* by Augustine, who wrote that concupiscence disperses the soul while the work of memory reassembles it.

The more specific meaning of *remembering* implies "reassembling the mind" in yet another way. We already saw that the aim that Freud assigned to psychoanalysis should not be reductively misunderstood as simply meaning to recall. If remembering implied the mere filling in of the blanks, we could hardly explain its mutative value, and, from a theoretical point of view, we would be prey of the "homunculus fallacy." Indeed, a "filling of the blanks" concept of remembering supposes a reader of the now more complete text—a reader external to the text itself. We should then imagine this reader *interpreting* the newly established script, and we would have to explain what makes him or her opt for one interpretation rather than another. This would introduce another level of functioning, which in turn would require some filling in followed by interpretation, and so on into infinite regress. On the contrary, remembering in the specific Freudian sense suggests that the subject is, so to speak, the remembered itself. By recomposing itself the soul also transforms itself. Remembering does not require an additional act of interpretation. Remembrance proper carries its own meaning, its own mutative force of conviction. To remember is to be able to say "I" again. "Wo Es war soll Ich werden. Es ist Kulturarbeit…" (Where id was, there ego shall be. A work of civilization…), Freud said.[8] This is not merely a technical observation, then; it carries some ethical issues in its wake, as we shall see.

Repetition and Binding

By providing a unified view in psychoanalysis, repetition can itself be seen as a principle, and in contrast with remembering, it is a principle operating "beyond the pleasure principle." I now wish to remind that this "beyond" is where the analytic work will usually take us, for better or for worse. *For better*, that is, if the compulsive mechanisms lying at the foundations of mental processes can, through analytic work, be put in a psychical form and thereby be processed according to the pleasure principle. A rewarding outcome, for certain, since, as we just saw, through remembering we obtain meaning, we insert delay and speech and therefore conscious thinking, in what tended to repeat itself compulsively. Although meaning can be painful at times, it is always preferable to meaningless repetition, as it opens the road to the highly desirable processes of mourning and symbolization, by which thinking is freer and more creative. This, I believe, is in line with Freud's discovery of 1919 that the most vital role of the psyche is to bind the quantity of excitation. Whenever such binding fails, mental functioning falls back on the stratum of repetition and *Agieren*, as these constitute the baseline or background functioning brought to the fore by the failure of symbolization. But while bringing repetition to the fore may seem the far worse outcome of the analytic endeavour, we know that it is often a road that the analysand must travel, as Freud's paper also indicates. One thing Freud does not indicate, however, is that repetition—or, if one prefers, unbinding—is provoked by the work of analysis itself. By dissolving the ready-made psychic constructions that the analysand brings to

---

8 Freud (1933 [1932]), p. 80.

analysis, we open the way to unbinding, although within the relatively secure framework of the analytic setting. Repetition eventually steps in as the "lower" and semi-failed form of the attempt at binding back or mastering the economic turmoil that such unbinding has caused. In this regard, repetition appears as the lower limit at which the unbinding resulting from analytic work can be contained without yielding to complete disorganization. Laplanche compares the analytic situation to that of a particle accelerator, where high energies are developed without risking a chain reaction, as with a nuclear bomb.[9]

Once again, the practical and theoretical consequences are quite important and carry in their wake major potential divergence from what we consider the proper work of psychoanalysis. When repetition steps in during psychoanalytic work, if one is not ready to consider it an intrinsic feature of the analysis, one can be drawn towards either despair or activism. I would go as far as to say that major revisions of the analytic stance that emerged in recent years are related to some form of activism occurring when we analysts are challenged by the outburst of non-psychical repetitive forms. Apparently, one is thereby simply struggling to keep the analytic work at the level of meaning, but we could contend that the activism in question results from our being ourselves subjected to the repetition principle in the counter-transference. In those instances, as the word *activism* itself suggests, remembering is bypassed in favour of action in both patient *and* analyst. This by no means implies that the analyst should never resort to any form of "enactment"; the unwarranted result I am pointing at is rather the systematic abandonment of the analytic method.

The Same and the Identical

I think it is useful at this point to bring in the important distinction Michel de M'Uzan once made between *repetition of the same*

---

9 Laplanche (1989 [1987])

and *repetition of the identical*.[10] Let's not be misled by the similarity of the terms. Repetition of the identical implies "true," or what I would call "radical" repetition, a repetition where no displacement or condensation, no primary process thinking occurs. It is doubtful that, except in fictional works, any human being could ever witness a true repetition of the identical. Even from a purely conceptual point of view, the philosophy of logic considers the notion of "identical" as a fundamental concept of thinking that cannot be itself defined.[11] At the empirical level, if we think of any situation in its entirety, the mere presence of the observer already inserts a major difference in any repeated event, no matter how close to the identical this may seem. Besides, the time frame of two separate observations of "identical" phenomena has necessarily changed the second time around. Thus, the notion of the identical is essentially a conceptual tool that helps us in thinking about the degrees of resemblance. At the level of experience, we are always left with *repetition of the same*.

For all the redundancy it carries in its wake, repetition of the same implies some form of novelty. Something is repeated, but a slight displacement, an almost unnoticeable nuance will in the long run significantly deviate the trajectory of what at first appeared to be perfect circularity. This aspect of repetition is what we may more promptly recognize in our clinical practice. Although for some time things seem to go desperately in circles, a small change in the tone of voice or a tiny detail in the narration becomes noticeable, and if we are sufficiently receptive to these events we may find that we are, so to speak, entering a different orbit, which reminds us that, dealing with the hyper-complex systems of the human body-mind, we cannot help but observe the kind of phenomena described in terms of non-linear dynamics. And although there is no need, nor for that matter the possibility, of doing any quantitative study of what matters in the

---

10 de M'Uzan (2004).
11 Lalande (1988 [1926]).

analytic session, there is no doubt that small deviations in the trajectory of the analysis at any given point may take us a long way.

As for repetition of the identical, it is not very distant from what Lacan called "the Real," in his theoretical trilogy (Symbolic, Imaginary, and Real). The Real was deemed by Lacan as that which, evading symbolization, always falls back in its place. Considering that displacement is, along with condensation, one of the primary thinking processes, the Real is what has not been or cannot be processed psychically, just like repetition of the identical. But despite its apparent distance from experience, we cannot avoid referring to repetition of the identical. We have already mentioned that the observable phenomena that in our field point to repetition are the *Agieren*—repetitions in action, outside of psychic elaboration. While repetition of the identical proper escapes empirical observation, it nevertheless introduces another clinically useful tool. Whereas a single *Agieren*, by standing outside of the psychical field, sufficed to identify repetition even in the absence of two comparable phenomena, the idea of repetition of the identical brings us one step further, since, in its wake, we need not even observe empirical action. Other clinical facts, indeed, hint at this sort of repetition. One classical example is the clinical syndrome Marty and de M'Uzan have called "operative thinking" (*pensée opératoire*), a condition that exposes the subject to serious psychic and/or somatic disorganization. In operative thinking, language is devoid of metaphors and slips of the tongue, sleep seems devoid of genuine dreaming, and the waking life of the patient is stuck in concreteness, lacking fantasy and daydreaming. One can assert that the thinking process is seriously hampered, although the concreteness may give the impression of strict realism. Repetition of the identical transpires here through the absence of displacement and the lack of imagination, which, if they existed, would launch the mind in creative mutations of forms and meanings.

But for all its peculiar aspects, this impoverished state of the mind should not, I believe, be restricted to psychopathological considerations. As with all pathology, in psychoanalysis we are called to look for its non-clinical form in the society as a whole. Thus, we may find a striking resemblance between the clinical picture I was just alluding to and what Hannah Arendt captured of the thinking processes in the criminal mind of Adolf Eichmann: "not stupidity, but a peculiar and genuine inaptitude for thinking. He functioned in his role of war criminal just in the same way he did under the Nazi regime: he had no problem whatsoever accepting a completely different set of rules."[12] These remarks seem to point, although from a different perspective, toward the notion of the identical. Indeed, in another part of her lecture, Arendt addresses precisely this point in remarking that as soon as one says "I," one is introducing a difference in oneself.[13] Saying "I" is precisely what Eichmann avoided doing, for it would have meant that instead of being the "law-abiding citizen" who carried out his duties and obeyed orders without ever questioning them, he would have been exerting his own thinking. He would, in other words, have been "remembering" instead of uncritically repeating in action; he would have "reassembled" his soul instead of having it complacently dispersed in the repetitive patterns of mass psychology. Mass psychology, indeed, is one form that the "legalized" psyche espouses when turning away from remembrance. I cannot go into more detail about this, but hope to have sufficiently underscored the moral and ethical aspects of what may seem a purely theoretical matter.

Repetition and Transference

Going back to clinical considerations, the metapsychological approach of repetition requires that we pay tribute to the identical (or the Real) as *the frontier at which genuine psychoanalytic work really happens*. The field of psychoanalysis is one where the territory is extended

---

12 Arendt (1996 [1970])
13 Arendt discusses the issue of identity and resemblance elsewhere in the same lecture I quote from, but I can't go into the details of her work here.

by the analytic work itself. One could almost speak of "psychoanalytic bootstrapping," were it not that it actually takes two to analyze, and therefore no "bootstrapping" is really happening. As a whole, however, the analytic situation can be compared to the building of a railway in some uncharted land, where it is the train itself that brings forth the workers and the material that will in turn bring the railway beyond the limits it had reached. J.-B. Pontalis writes that psychoanalysis does not simply dwell inside a ready-made psychic space but rather works towards *instituting* the psychic space itself. "The reality of psychoanalysis can reside only at the limits of the analyzable."[14]

Ordinarily, transference is deemed the prototypical form of repetition in analysis. As it is one of the shibboleths of psychoanalysis, it may seem, well…redundant to speak of transference in this context, but, in spite of the vast literature on this topic, I can't possibly avoid saying a few things here. In the paper I just quoted, Pontalis warns against constantly interpreting "transference" when what is actually happening is a repetition in act (*"une répétition agie"*).[15] This may seem surprising at first: isn't transference a clear instance of repetition, as suggested by Freud when he writes, "We soon notice that transference is in itself nothing else than a fragment of repetition and that repetition is the transference of the forgotten past not only on the physician but also on every other domain of the present situation?"[16] What I find remarkable here is that when Freud defines transference as a fragment of repetition, he clearly implies that not all repetition is transference. Conversely, when he adds that repetition is the transference of the forgotten past, he gives transference a much larger extension than is usually the case today. This extension is also noticeable in other papers from the same period, such as "The Dynamics of Transference," where he mentions transference on the health care

---

14 Pontalis (1974), p. 15. (My translation, emphasis in the original).
15 Op. cit.
16 Freud (1914a), p. 190. (My translation).

institution as a whole.[17] To be sure, we would impoverish the notion of transference if we did not listen to its literal meaning, which implies displacement or transport. This immediately suggests that what we usually refer to as transference in the analytic setting is but a subset of the general phenomenon of displacement. Displacement, then, is the wider, more encompassing category we are called upon to include in our study of repetition and transference. We have already touched upon displacement when we mentioned that repetition of the identical is equivalent to Lacan's Real, something that falls back in its place, that was not displaced. On the other hand, we saw that some displacement is necessarily at work in repetition of the same.

Let us now go back to the apparent discrepancy between Freud's views and those of Pontalis when he states that the analyst should not insist on interpreting as transference what is really a repetition in action. We can understand better what Pontalis had in mind if we posit that interpretable transference usually relates to repetition of the same, while repetition in action is closer to repetition of the identical. This is tantamount to saying that usually transference interpretations regard what is already in the domain of meaning, albeit in a preconscious state, while what is repeated in action does not yield immediate meaning and therefore should not, as Pontalis points out, be "filled in with interpretations that are only a response to the vacuum, the hollowing out felt [by the analyst]."[18]

Jean Laplanche has also formulated, although from a different perspective, a clear-cut difference between what he calls "filled-in" and "hollowed-out" transference.[19] While making no manifest reference to repetition itself, I believe that what Laplanche has in mind revolves around this very issue. "Filled-in transference" refers to phenomena in the analysis (words, dreams, memories, feelings, etc.) that can be traced back to situations in the analysand's accessible, represented

---

17 Freud (1912).
18 Pontalis (1974), p. 13. (My translation).
19 Laplanche (1989 [1987]).

past. When, for instance, the analysand brings a dream that clearly connects something the analyst said to words spoken by the patient's father or mother during his childhood, even though we can't always immediately grasp the meaning of this connection, we know and feel that we are dwelling in an area where meaning is within reach. The elements at hand share among them the same psychic status. Repetition in such an instance means resemblance, and the link between present and past exists also on the basis of a common temporal background. The past is already there as past, and while the present shares with such a past a number of connecting points that can be uncovered by the analysis, it will often result in this being only a preliminary work, setting the stage for more impervious material to come. Regarding this other kind of material, what is particular is that it could not be elicited by previous knowledge, neither by the patient nor the analyst. This is where Laplanche speaks of "hollowed-out" transference, a form of transference by which the analysand unknowingly deposits not some "positive" content, but rather his actualized relationship to the enigma of his infancy. The hollowed-out form of the transference is itself deposited in another hollow, the one the analyst provides by firmly holding to her "refusal to know"—refusal to "bind" the analysand in the chains of the analyst's preconceptions."[20] Such refusal is both technically required and ethically mandatory for the analyst, insofar as analysis is aimed at opening new mental spaces for the analysand rather than yielding yet another interpretation of what was more readily reachable.[21] The unforeseen is, so to speak, what the analytic dyad was struggling to reach by operating within a thoroughly analytic framework. As we saw earlier, it is the very work of analysis that is responsible for the unbinding conducive to repetition of the identical, from where the work of binding/ remembering may resume.

---

20 Laplanche (1999 [1991]).
21 In this respect, we would need to discuss in depth the difference between repetition in Freud's "Remembering, repeating and working-through" and repetition in Freud's *Beyond the Pleasure Principle,* but time and space do not allow.

Repetition and Time

From still another perspective, we are reminded of Winnicott's "Fear of Breakdown." In this case the repetition in the transference concerns something that was not experienced because "the ego [was] too immature to gather all the phenomena into the area of personal omnipotence."[22] The clinical situation Winnicott has in mind is one where, "if the patient is ready for some kind of acceptance of this queer kind of truth, that what is not yet experienced did nevertheless happen in the past, then the way is open for the agony to be experienced in the transference, in reaction to the analyst's failures."[23] When Winnicott speaks of something that was never experienced, I hear "not reproduced in the psychical field," and therefore belonging to repetition. This implies that the repetition in question is happening to the analytic couple for the first time. This "first time" must be taken literally, meaning that *time itself* is entering the scene "for the first time." Time is catching hold of something that, as Winnicott himself writes, "cannot get into the past tense unless the ego can first gather it into its own present time experience and into omnipotent control now."[24] This is most interesting: Winnicott is writing of something that must have happened but was never registered within the time dimension: it is therefore not present or past, since it can be put "into the past tense" only if some conditions are realized.

Thus, we now have one more way of defining repetition in analysis, especially the kind of repetition closer to the identical: a repetition is what has not yet been given a "time tag," so to speak, what has not yet been inserted into chronology or belongs to the category sometimes referred to as "actual time."[25] What is "actual" in "actual

---

22 Winnicott (1989 [1964]).
23 Op. cit.
24 Op. cit.
25 Scarfone (2006a). This volume chapter 1.

time" gets into the "present tense" by being experienced "now," and only then can it be "put into the past tense." Therefore we can assert that while repetition, when looked at from a third-person point of view, seems to bring back something "from the past," this is not accurate. From the point of view of both analyst and analysand, repetition is actually bringing in something *not yet belonging to the past*, because it was *not yet marked by time*.

This is in line with an important technical guideline in *Remembering, Repeating and Working-Through*. Freud writes that "we must treat the illness not as something related to history but as a presently active force," but he immediately adds that "while the patient experiences [the morbid state] as something real and present, we must carry out the therapeutic work, a good part of which consists in driving matters back to the past."[26] One way of understanding these precepts is that, according to what we have just seen in Winnicott, important things repeat themselves in analysis that are *not yet part of the patient's history*. Here again, the peculiar nature of repetition in analysis makes it something different from what common sense would suggest. Moreover, Freud's definition of remembering as "reproduction in the psychical field" and his dynamic point of view by which remembering corresponds to "lifting the resistance of repression" must be once more taken into account. Since the repressed unconscious is deemed by Freud as *"Zeitlos"*—lacking the dimension of time—then his precept of "driving matters back to the past" entails *actually instituting the category of the past*. It is, again, a matter of inserting chronological time into the "actuality" of repetition. While the past to which present matters must be driven back could be plainly (and erroneously) conceived of as the series of events bygone, it must be thought of as the *psychic category* towards which our work must drive the actual—or, in Freud's words "timeless"—unconscious facts. Those facts, as we saw, take place in analysis "for the first time," hence,

---

26 Winnicott (1989 [1964]), p. 191.

they do not "emerge" from the past; they were *brought into presence* and out of their "actuality" (timelessness) by their repetition in the transference.[27]

Between Meaning and Presence

The phrase I just used, "brought into presence," requires some clarification. By "presence" I am not referring to some "here-and-now" technique in analysis.[28] I hope everything I said up until now was able to convey that the "presence" in question has little to do with the ahistorical, or even anti-historical stance implied in the "here-and-now" technique. For one thing, the "here-and-now" attitude rests on the assumption that the past does not really matter, that what counts is the interaction between patient and analyst as "real persons" evolving in the present tense of a "real" relationship.[29] Regarding the question of the past, not only is it important, from my perspective, but I actually uphold the idea that one major aim of psychoanalysis is to institute the psychic category of the past. Obviously this implies that the past is not some passive repository of static recordings, but a living psychic domain where *Nachträglichkeit* is at work, where psychic elaboration has retroactive effects on what the past will bear, and, in turn, the creation and nurturing of the past has a stabilizing effect on the functioning of the psyche as a whole. Therefore, "bringing into presence" through repetition in the transference is in no way a repudiation of the past. Quite the contrary.

As for the possible conflation of the idea of "presence" with that of the analyst and analysand as "real persons" engaging in a "real

---

27 Scarfone (2006a). This volume chapter 1.
28 For an inspiring reflection about presence vs. meaning, see Gumbrecht (2003).
29 A thorough treatment of this topic would require a specific discussion of difficult issues regarding time, the notions of "present" and "past," as well as the idea of the "flow of time." I obviously cannot delve into these difficult matters here. For a partial discussion of this, see Scarfone (2006a). This volume chapter 1.

relationship," one must first consider what lies underneath the word *real*. Obviously, when there is talk of "real persons" in analysis today, one does not mean to suggest that there would otherwise be phantoms or zombies in the analytic room. What the advocates of "getting real" do is overtly trade the analytic method of free association and evenly suspended attention for a more "ordinary dialogue," even containing a measure of self-disclosure on the part of the analyst.[30] It would take too much of the allotted space here to indicate the extent of my disagreement with these views. Here I simply want to be more explicit about the status of the "presence" I am referring to, and its relationship with repetition.

Many say that psychoanalysis was really born when Freud abandoned the theory of seduction in 1897 and instead gave priority to unconscious fantasy as the main object of psychoanalytic inquiry. The story is of course debatable, but the fact remains that the prototypical work of analysis puts the absent or lost object at its core, the vicissitudes of affect and representation being what the analytic work is supposed to deal with primarily. This is certainly correct in describing where we start from in our analytic endeavour, but it is insufficient if it implies that all of psychoanalysis is concerned with meaning, a concealed meaning that is there for us to discover in a permutation of representations. One could argue, indeed, that from 1914 on, turning his attention to repetition and the repetition compulsion, Freud began dealing with a region of the mind where representation is not the crux of the matter anymore. This culminates, as is well known, in "Beyond the Pleasure Principle" and "The Ego and the Id," where a new model of the mind is proposed, with a non-representational id making for the bulk of the mind, while ego and superego stand as differentiated subsets thereof. We need not, however, take sides for or against this new model in order to see that this is not so much a departure from previous views as a new way of presenting some ideas that may have

---

30 Renik (1999).

been lost sight of.³¹ What looks at first like a discovery is actually, well . . . a repetition in a new guise of something that came from Freud's pen at different periods of his creative path. I am alluding to the many faces of what lies "beyond"—or, if one prefers, this side of—representation, beyond one of the three elements that Freud's teacher in philosophy, Franz Brentano, had probably taught him to look for. In line with the philosophical tradition of Thomas Aquinas, Brentano thought that three things populate the mind: affects, representations, and judgments. Not surprisingly, then, we can retrieve these elements embedded in some of the major tenets of Freud's theory, where affects and representations are the two psychic delegates (or representatives) of the drives, while repression is described as a preliminary form of judgment, halfway between the impossible flight from the drives' pressure and the as yet-unattainable full judgment of condemnation.³²

Freud was never merely a psychologist, and one reason why he coined the term *metapsychology* is that he hoped that his theory would provide a biological as much as a psychological explanation of mental phenomena.³³ Representations must then have smacked too much of psychologism to someone who wished to develop a scientific psychology. And so it is that, throughout Freud's works, we find reference to what lies beyond representation, beyond the strictly psychological grasp of the life of the mind. In the 1895 *Project for a Scientific Psychology*, for instance, just when he is dealing with the highly psychological themes of cognition, reproductive thought, remembering, and judging,³⁴ Freud speaks in some detail of one major "perceptual complex" he calls "the complex of the fellow human being." He writes that this complex "falls apart into two components,

---

31 I here stand on the shoulders of Laplanche (1987) who expounded this idea in relation to the death drive as a rediscovery of "demonic" sexuality after the introduction of narcissism and Eros.
32 Freud (1915b).
33 "Letter of March 10, 1898" in "The Complete Letters of Freud to Fliess" (1985).
34 Freud (1895a), Ch. 16 and 17 of part 1.

of which one makes an impression by its constant structure and stays together as a *thing* [*Ding*], while the other can be *understood* by the activity of memory—that is can be traced back to information from [the subject's] own body."[35] By calling upon the work of memory and one's own bodily experience, the "understanding" clearly implies a *transformation* occurring in the representation of the other through the experience of self. Such a processing of perception that travels through the filters of memory and is modified accordingly, while preserving something of the perceived other, amounts to a reproduction of *the same* or instates *the remembered other*, as I would have it. By contrast, what strikes us in the "thing"—in what eludes judgment or understanding—is that it "makes an impression by its constant structure." So here we are in 1895, looking at the roots of what Freud was to explore in more detail in 1914: a "reproduction in the psychical field," which is *Erinnerung* or remembering, as opposed to something that makes an impression by way of its constant structure, belonging to the realm of repetition, actually quite close to de M'Uzan's "repetition of the identical." In other words, what "makes an impression" or "imposes itself" unchanged, and escapes understanding, is what cannot be processed by the work of remembering nor filtered by the experience of self. It is what cannot be put inside (*er-innern*) when the soul reassembles itself. The *thing* is not represented but rather *imposes* itself, *presents* itself, outside of reproductive thinking.

Other instances of the same idea can be found in areas as diverse as dream theory and the psychopathology of the neuroses. I am referring here, for example, to what Freud mentions twice in his dream book of 1900, that every dream contains an umbilicus, something by which it is "connected to what is not known." Here then, at the core of the most appropriate material for analysis—the dream—Freud remarks that some hard kernel stands in the way of our hope to fully analyze it. This limitation, it must be noted, is not due to some

---

35 Op. cit., p. 331.

relativistic point of view regarding the many possible interpretations of a dream. Freud is clearly speaking of—and our clinical experience confirms—the existence of something in the dream that is utterly non-interpretable, something that, in the terms of our present discussion, can be said to stand outside of remembering. A nucleus of repetition lies at the core of the most elaborate dream. Yet another instance of "presence" at the center of the representational world is the kernel of "actual neurosis" that Freud posited as lying within many if not all "psychoneuroses."[36]

In conclusion, I wish to underscore one important aspect of the relationship between remembering and repeating that I have left aside. I said at the beginning that repetition appears wherever there is a failure in remembering. But, for all its usefulness at the clinical level, this is a rather judgmental view of repetition. From a strictly metapsychological point of view, repetition clearly stands not simply as a degraded form of remembering but also as an important source of novelty for the mind. This sounds at first like a blatant contradiction! How could repetition, and even more so, repetition of the identical, be a source of novelty? I would be taxing your attention too much if I now went into the details of this final aspect. Let me just go back briefly to the presence of repetition that is felt—and often can only be suspected—*in the midst of remembering*, as a kernel of material that was not yet, or could not, be processed by the work of memory. This is not very distant conceptually from the notion of *resistance*, which, over more than a century of psychoanalytic work and reflection, we have learned to consider as both the major hindrance in the work of analysis and yet the most necessary ingredient for analysis to happen. While resistance is, still today, all too often negatively connoted, it nevertheless provides the only solid foundation for analytic work, if by this we mean not merely translating from one set of represen-

---

36 Freud (1933 [1932])

tations to another, but the actual creation of meaning out of what was not yet amenable to representing, understanding, or genuine thinking. As Freud's paper of 1914 clearly shows, a conceptual circle formed by repetition, transference, and resistance stands out at the level of clinical experience. But we need only dig a bit deeper towards the metapsychological layer, to see that "repetition of the identical," the "umbilicus of the dream," the "kernel of actual neurosis," and the "thing" give us a more detailed idea of what psychoanalytic work is about. As Pontalis said, analysis happens only at the limits of the analyzable, that is, where resistance is the greatest. The work of analysis is therefore not so much a work of *uncovering* as a work of *extracting* thinking out of repetition—a work that requires remembering, understood as the reassembling of the mind. It is a genuine production of meaning out of what our fiercest foe and most secret ally, repetition, brings into presence in the analytic situation.

In the Hollow of Transference: The Analyst's Position Between Activity and Passivity*

In response to Sitegeist's *kind invitation to take part in this special issue celebrating the work of Jean Laplanche, it seems obvious to me that a panegyric of the man and his work is uncalled for. The best way to pay tribute to both man and work instead consists in undertaking what Laplanche himself has always advocated: putting his thought to work again. This modest contribution pays homage to a master who is not only responsible for a renewal of psychoanalytical thought: through his teaching and the example he has set, Laplanche has succeeded in prompting each psychoanalyst to think for herself or himself, bequeathing a method conducive to a better engagement in and a safeguarding of the freedom thus yielded. This article is inscribed in the wake of Laplanche's developments in a key text on transference, "Transference: Its Provocation by the Analyst,"[1] with its specific focus on the analyst's position. Relying on the work of Emmanuel Levinas and Jean-François Lyotard, I argue that the position of the analyst—who is active insofar as his enigma and his refusals provoke transference—presupposes an inherent fundamental passivity—or possibility—without which the provocation of transference would fail to provide simultaneously the 'hollow' required for its deployment.*

---

1 (Laplanche, 1999 [1991a])

*This paper was originally published in Sitegeist, #4, Spring 2010

Jean Laplanche teaches us how to read Freud and, in his own reading of Freud, he outlines a theory of general seduction—or, alternatively, a general theory of seduction—that maps out a crucial context within which to theorize both the human condition and psychoanalytic practice. *The human condition* since Laplanche identifies a dimension of reality that is specific to it: the reality of the message as it emerges in the fundamental anthropological situation, constituted by the asymmetry characteristic of the *infans*'s confrontation with the adult world as bearer of unconscious *sexual*;[2] *analytic practice*, insofar as this message is endowed with a sexual reality that is marked by repression. The translation of this message, already attempted by the analysand, must be undone in the analytical setting, in order to open up the possibility of a new translation. These two crucial dimensions are also present in Laplanche's acknowledgment that the person we are most concerned with in human communication is the second person. *Not* the person whom I speak to but, above all, the person who speaks to *me*, the person before whom I am in a state of fundamental *passivity*; this term does not denote a form of behaviour but a relationship in which the other's message contains something extra, some excess. For my part, I have long opted, in the matter, for the term suggested by Lyotard, i.e. *passibility*, because it profitably does away with the ambiguity as to the kind of passivity at stake. However one could equally refer to Levinas when he evokes a 'passivity (…) more passive still than any receptivity',[3] a passivity that therefore precedes any kind of deliberate or forced passivation, a primal passivity that holds us hostage to the other, besieged, persecuted. Levinas's account resonates quite unambiguously with Laplanche's suggestion that man stands

---

2 Translator's note: 'sexual' refers to Laplanche's use of the German term sexual, which Laplanche distinguishes from the French term sexuel and denotes an expanded view of sexuality in the light of Freud's theory. See Jean Laplanche, *Freud and the Sexual*, The Unconcious in Translation (2011[2007]).
3 Levinas, 1991 [1978]: 48

'between seduction and inspiration', with persecution lodged in this in-between.[4]

Just as Levinas never brought psychoanalysis into play, Laplanche has not drawn on Levinas's philosophy and the kind of persecution Laplanche is concerned with in his writings has more to do with Schreber than with man in general.[5] But only a view of psychosis as an extra-human phenomenon would fail to see how persecution, hyperbolized as it is in its delusional expression, seems fundamentally tied to the human condition. The other speaks to me and his words haunt me, excite me, incite me, inspire me, with or without my knowledge. Freud did not miss the contiguity of theory and delusion when reading Schreber's memoirs. Such contiguity is equally confirmed by the fact that what the theory of seduction foregrounds through complex theoretical efforts is generally perceived by psychotics in a seemingly more direct and concrete way. The former efforts consist in a deconstruction of certain pivotal moments in Freud and in the patient 'stabbing the knife' into the various epicycles that psychoanalytic theory began to require, once its Copernican revolution was overlooked.

When the de-centering carried out by Freud's theory of seduction was replaced by a recentering on fantasy—conceived of in terms of the first person singular—psychoanalysts actually set out to find a construction of reality on the basis of the 'egocentered' position that was subsequently devolved on the subject. Fantasy is hardly insignificant in psychoanalytic practice or in the psychic reality arising from the theory of seduction which posits a process of radical decentering.

---

[4] Aware of the differences at work between these two authors, I am drawing the above parallel with some hesitation. As I was writing this paper, I came across some of Judith Butler's work (2005) that explores various aspects of the con-nections between Laplanche and Levinas. Due to a lack of space and time, I could not go into the details of Butler's arguments in the context of the present paper, but my understanding is that my conclusions differ from Butler's regarding the possible compatibility of Laplanche's and Levinas's reflections.
[5] Laplanche, 1999 [1999a]

Laplanche's theory, however, is critical of the fact that, as a result of the theoretical recentering on fantasy, the origin of the latter seems unaccountably neglected—or relegated to innateness—if one fails to see it as a response to the reality of the message and its enigma. This reality is thus primary and not in need of being constructed; however enigmatic, it is a prior reality in relation to which fantasy constitutes a form of subjective engagement. This subjective engagement must be addressed by the analyst with all the respect due to the freedom bestowed on each and every one when translating the other's enigma for oneself. Otherwise, the risk is of partaking in a kind of 'objectivism' likely to smother all forms of individuality. In this sense, the analyst's intervention does not address fantasy. Rather, the analyst assists the analysand in the necessary deconstruction of fantasy, insofar as the subjective positioning achieved until then and crystalized in a fantasmatic scene has led the subject to an impasse that underlies the demand for analysis.

In this short essay, I would like to explore in more details the second-person position, that of the person who speaks to me, in the sense that the one who 'is spoken to' is not only the subject requesting an analysis, but is also embodied by the analyst himself. For it seems clear that the analyst is expressly positioned as the one who is spoken to in the second-person and who is, consequently, in a state of relative passivity. This position, unless I am mistaken, has not been explored yet by the theory of general seduction. Indeed, in this theory of general seduction, the analyst is active because his enigma yields the provocation of transference.[6] If the analysand positions the analyst as 'the subject who is supposed to know', that is because from his own position as 'guardian of the enigma', the analyst is the bearer of an 'excess of message', an excess that triggers a process of translation-detranslation, of transferential projections and fantasizations, whose elaboration, in the course of the analytic session, might

---

6 Laplanche, 1999 [1991a]

elicit the advent of some form of unbinding—the prelude to less rigid reconstructions of meaning. This essentially consists in a process of mourning, mourning that does not 'liquidate', but carries out a process of unweaving-reweaving, a re-reading of the other's message, a re-interpretation.[7] However, this marks a return to a hermeneutic position featuring, this time, the encounter between a subjectivity that was until now unaware of having any active role in the preceding interpretations and a reality that could not be located in the proper place, i.e. the place of the message left by the other. The acknowledgment of this reality, in hermeneutic solitude, will elicit the emergence of the other's trace, a trace stamped by the repressed that operated in him, just as it already operated in the issuer. In short, under Laplanche's magnifying glass, the analytic situation reinstates this connection to the other's message. As the analyst holds the pole of activity, the refounding of the analytic space first pertains to him and his 'refusals'.

So let us precisely start from the analyst's refusals, in order to examine more closely how his position evolves in the context of the session, once such refusals have been embraced. For example, I would regard the mere advocacy of the active refusal to know as insufficient, unless one sees how it coincides with a basic form of passivity in the analyst himself. For while the analyst may actively refuse to know or act, this refusal stems from a position of withdrawal which would be unthinkable as the mere effect of a technique, cut off from any relation to the primal passivity that applies to analyst and analysand alike. Such passivity precedes—even though the issue of situating it in time is not at stake—the passivity before the message of primal seduction; it is not a return to something ancient but it consists instead in the reactualization of an ever present predicament: i.e. the fact of being besieged, persecuted, held hostage by the other, as one might posit following Emmanuel Levinas.

---

7 Laplanche, 1999 [1991b

The Unpast

I make this link with Levinas's thought not as a philosopher—which I am not[8] but as an analyst. I am bound to notice that, if I provoke transference thanks to the 'excess of message' embedded in the enigma that emanates from my own unconscious in my desire to analyze, by the same token I nonetheless surrender to the 'grip' of transference, I expose myself to a kind of 'possession'. The displacement onto me—the result of having accepted being the receptacle of what is being transferred—leads me to substantiate the human condition's accusative mode in general, which is relocated and foregrounded here by the additional constraint operating within the framework of the analysis. It would consequently be reductive to tackle this effect as a simple artefact of psychoanalytic technique. Such propensity to possession converges with the typically Kleinian account that posits the analyst as the recipient of the transferred objects (my point here is not discuss whether this takes place through projective identification or not). This is another possible illustration of the human position as passible, an actualization, for the benefit of the analysis, of the basic passivity-passibility that any person encounters when facing the other. Such a position does not result from a technique; it emerges, conversely, as the very condition that elicits the analytic method itself, provided the two protagonists, in the course of an analysis, are tacitly required to carry out an *épochè*, a suspension of their ego, a departure from their ego-centered position. The analysand is prompted to associate as 'freely' as possible; the analyst is to sustain an equally free-floating form of attention. These two stances do not complement each other. According to Freud, they operate on two different stages.[9] Yet they both rely on a general disposition that must be recaptured through a specific effort, which goes against the grain

---

8 I am indebted to Professor Bettina Bergo, my colleague in the Department of Philosophy at the University of Montreal, for shedding such a helpful light on Levinas's thought. However, she is not to be held accountable for my understanding of this author.
9 Freud 1937b

of natural inclination. The fact that access to such disposition requires an effort against the grain comes from the need to accommodate a more basic position with which the ego is constantly confronted. This clearly resonates with the 'underlying bedrock' discussed by Freud in the conclusion of his text 'Analysis Terminable and Interminable'.[10] Whereas Freud relies, when accounting for the process of ultimate resistance, on differentiated forms following the man/woman split (i.e. the refusal of passive submission to the father and penis envy, respectively), one could arguably envision this resistance as based on a common stratum. The latter consists in the refusal of primordial passivity insofar as this refusal is a process of closure to the other, to the other's impact, to the other's message. According to Laplanche, the enigma in the other's message is seen as the quasi empirical outcome of the adult-*infans* asymmetry regarding the *sexual*. Yet, seemingly, one could and should consider this *sexual* at another level, because the mere inclusion of the empirical field implicitly refers to a developmental theory. On the contrary, it is highly relevant to envision a level of transcendence—following a very Laplanchian line of reasoning in the process: the other who speaks to me, haunts me, obsesses and persecutes me is the other of the *sexual*, which emerges as the paradigm of *any* encounter where the issuer is equally caught up in the infantile (the *sexual*) within. In this sense, where Levinas posits that the other's face commands, 'Do not kill me!', one could legitimately infer a reference to Laplanche's *sexual*, 'Do not force your way in, do not rape me!'.

Inserting the *sexual* into a Levinassian context may seem incongruous but there are arguments in support of such a connection with psychoanalysis. For instance, when Levinas is asked to give an example of the '*there is*' in an interview with Philippe Nemo, he ends up describing no other than a primal scene! First he evokes a childhood memory: "One sleeps alone, the adults continue life; the child

---

10 Freud, 1937a

feels the silence of his bedroom as 'rumbling.'".[11] And as if the pregnance of the sexual scene implied by the term 'rumbling' were not obvious enough, Levinas further evokes related notions borrowed from his friend Maurice Blanchot. "He [Blanchot] has a number of very suggestive formulas: he speaks of the 'hustle-bustle' of being, of its 'clamor,' its 'murmur.' A night in a hotel room where, behind the partition, 'it does not stop stirring'; 'one does not know what they are doing next door.' This is something very close to the 'there is.'"[12] And very close, let us add, to a seduction scene *par excellence*! This connection would nonetheless be a dreadful reduction if, in reading a primal scene into Levinas's illustration of the 'there is', we would claim to explain away this 'there is' on the basis of the sexual scene. This is not what is at stake. The point, rather, is to see how the primal scene itself is the representable form of a 'thing' that is impossible to describe otherwise than in an impersonal form: i.e. the 'there is' for Levinas, the enigmatic in the message adulterated by the *sexual* for Laplanche, or, one might add, *das Ding* mentioned by Freud in the *Project* and revisited by Lacan in his Ethics Seminar.[13] What is at stake, in any case, is something impossible to master or translate completely into a familiar representation, something which, besides, exposes our primordial passivity. This passivity is opposed by the ego that becomes, in the process, all the more entrapped in the effects of that 'thing' as its resistance to otherness reinforces the rigidity of the *Same*.[14] In an analysis, if the attempt to suspend the ego is in any way successful, a more flexible and inclusive symbolization will ultimately emerge, without any claim to exhaust the enigma of the other's message. This is achieved, in any case, through a re-opening of the fundamental anthropological situation, through a reinstatement of the *infans*'s position of passivity.

---

11 Levinas, 1985 [1982]: 48
12 Levinas, 1985 [1982], 49-50
13 Lacan, 1959-60
14 Levinas often uses 'Same' to refer to the Ego, a designation psychoanalysis can easily endorse.

In the Hollow of Transference

It seems to me that Levinas's claims also point in the same direction when, in the interview quoted above, he concludes: "to escape the 'there is' one must not be posed but deposed; to make an act of deposition, in the sense one speaks of deposed kings. This deposition of sovereignty by the ego is the social relationship with the Other (…)."[15]

In a given analysis, if the re-opening of the fundamental anthropological situation places the analysand before the analyst's enigma, thus prompting transference, the analyst, according to Laplanche, still offers a 'hollow' for this transference, a holding capacity (*contenance*).[16] How can one conceive of this 'hollow' bestowed by the analyst upon the analysand? Where could the analyst find such a hollow within himself if he did not 'deposing' his own ego in order to recapture a primordial disposition which, though generally unnoticed in everyday life, is called upon in exquisite fashion in the disposition for analytic listening? In this sense, one could argue that the opening carried out by the instatement and the reinstatement of the analytic situation presents itself as a philosophy in action, or rather, as the methodically performed actualization of an ethical stance that would be termed psychoanalysis. Such ethics is also our epistemics, granting access to facts that would otherwise remain unavailable to our experience.

In fact, the analyst's function as 'the one who provokes transference' would be utterly intolerable if such active re-opening of the fundamental anthropological situation did not simultaneously comprise the signs of a proper deposition of the analyst's ego, of his being 'caught up' within the very situation. In other words, the analyst does not merely and empirically reinstate the adult-child asymmetry which the analysand once experienced. This asymmetry is not only historical: it transcends the dateable empirical fact in yet another way, insofar as the analyst remains caught up in it, in his personal reality as a human being as well as in his specifically analytic positioning.

---

15 Levinas, 1985 [1982]: 52
16 Laplanche, 1999 [1991a]

The Unpast

The provocation of transference by the analyst is in fact not traumatic since, unlike what happens in the case of ordinary seduction and even more so in the case of perverse seduction—the analyst's active part is doubled up by the hollow he bestows in order to host transference, a kind of hospitality that echoes the primordial passivity evoked by Levinas. Without granting primacy to such passivity-passibility, without becoming the actual hostage of the transferential hold, the analyst would only be able to *comprehend*, not *hear*. Despite the positive value it may present at the outset, understanding 'refers back to an act of grasping', as Levinas suggests.[17] It implies a grip, a control, a seizure.

Analytic practices in which the analyst essentially puts himself in charge of interpreting, i.e. of translating on behalf of the patient the words uttered by the latter, are rightfully subject to criticism in the light of their subjectivist and relativist potential. So much so that some authors, in the United States in particular, have simply given up in the face of this apparently unavoidable aspect of the analytic practice and have willfully embraced their 'irreducible subjectivity'. But the result has been a discarding of any claim to analytic neutrality and an advocacy of the psychological self-disclosure of the analyst in the course of the session.[18] I believe the origins of this drift may be seen as a reaction to the traditionally hermeneutic position adopted by analysts, a position which, in its extreme form, has yielded the figure of the omniscient analyst. The theory of general seduction, combined with a translation model of mental functioning, is sited against the grain of both aforementioned positions. It places the analysand in charge of the hermeneutic work while the orientation of the analyst's work is anti-hermeneutic.[19] Yet, such anti-hermeneutics cannot, in my opinion, be reduced to a purely negative activity. In other words, the

---

17 Levinas, 1989: 76
18 among others, see Renik, 2004
19 Laplanche, 1999b

analyst cannot merely refuse to know or understand. *Hearing* presupposes a greater form of openness: what is to be heard has to do with a quality in communication whose comprehension is only graspable on the side of the *Same*, whereas the encounter summoning both analyst and analysand is the encounter with the *other*. Hearing implies welcoming the analysand's speech without immediately reducing the latter to an assured 'I hear you'; it implies allowing the alien-ness that dwells in that speech to run its course, through the analyst's attempt to depose, if not revoke, his own ego. The analyst's aural offering thus denotes a disposition in which attention cannot be exclusively paid to signifiers, insofar as the other's speech, received in a state of passibility, is to give way to felt experiences in the analyst, leading to perceptible changes in his listening. It is a matter of states—the states in which the analyst finds himself—which are somewhat reminiscent of what was referred to as possession during the pre-Freudian era. It is the 'grip of transference', a grip from which the analyst will have to disentangle himself, but whose advent he must first allow for.[20] This grip means that analytic listening cannot claim to be immune to the reorientations resulting from the particular transference of a particular analysand. The analyst's active part in the reinstatement of the originary enigma is therefore doubled up by the analyst's essential passivity-passibility: through his listening disposition, he agrees to be affected on a very different plane than the relatively controllable plane of understanding.

In his formulations, Jean Laplanche has hesitated between the terms 'enigmatic signifiers', 'enigmatic messages' or 'compromised messages'. Regarding signifiers, he has nonetheless specified that he mostly retains the fact of their address, the fact that they 'signify to'. So far as the other's message is concerned, then it cannot be a question of keeping to signifiers alone, linguistically or semiologically

---

20 Gantheret, 1996

speaking. For my part, I would add that, in the other's message, all is not addressed either. Jean François Lyotard does not discuss messages but rather is interested in phrases as irreducible units.[21] Phrases, on the one hand, consist of a content which is, say, semantic (*lexis*); on the other hand, they include a *phônè* which is located in the sonority, the grain of the voice, in the tone.[22] In the phrase regime, Lyotard foregrounds the existence of an affect-phrase which is not a phrase strictly speaking;[23] it is transmitted but not addressed or formed according to any grammar or syntax appropriate for signification—it neither 'signifies that' nor 'signifies to'. Applied to the psychoanalytic sphere, this would refer, as I understand it, to whatever emerges from a more originary source than the adult's repressed, the repressed which, in the theory of seduction, contaminates the message intercepted by the *infans*. For example, this is what causes the aesthetic experience passed on by the painter and which one encounters in front of a painting. The affect-phrase is inarticulate; furthermore, 'the encounter between articulated phrase and affect-phrase can only be a missed encounter'.[24] The analyst's listening, made liable to influence because of its passivity, paradoxically imposes an address on what is not necessarily meant to be heard—because it was not addressed, even unconsciously. Listening in passibility consequently does some violence to the phrase because it commandeers the phrase, so to speak, turning it into a transferential address.[25] But this necessary violence—the violence of the passivity-passibility—is the violence that unveils the indissoluble link that speech ties between the *Same* and the other; it also discloses the inevitable reference to something beyond meaning that transcends any form of understanding, leading the analyst to welcome without mastering. As previously seen, the welcoming host

---

21 Lyotard, 1983
22 Lyotard, 1991
23 Lyotard, 2000
24 Lyotard, 2000: 47
25 Scarfone, 2008

is a hostage: he is caught up, possessed. His act of welcoming is nonetheless able to transform what he receives, through the imposition of an address on what originally had no addressee. It is the listener's responsibility, however, to position his act of listening so as to refrain from exerting secondary violence against the intercepted phrase;[26] in other words, he must keep only to what is exactly called for in order to send back to the speaker the hint of another phrase, so far unbeknownst to him.

A question emerges at once: does this act of listening that imposes an address not open, after all, the path for some arbitrariness in the interpretation? What would be the extent of our departure from the analyst-as-hermeneut if our analyst-as-hostage presented himself as the expert interpreter of the inarticulate? This is, I believe, the locus of one of the analyst's refusals, which Laplanche posits as the condition for the establishment and the sustainability of the analytical situation. More specifically, the point will consist, in the present case, in knowing how to take account of the peripatetic elements in the world of phrases, without, however, making the analysand answerable for what he could not put into words. What would then be the point of listening to the non-articulated, one might ask? The point will be to modulate the listening modalities of the translations generated by the analysand, prompting the two protagonists in the course of the session to pay attention to what would otherwise not be featured 'in person' in the analysis. The non-articulated phrase evoked by Lyotard, an adjunct to the *logos* without being reduced to it, is a reminder that the bottom-line in the issue of the unconscious does not pertain to representation but to presentation; not language but a-phasia, a speechless voice. Such presentation is to occur provided the process of de-translation at work during the session—i.e. the deconstruction of the formations produced by the subject in response to the other's enigmatic message—is not a process of a cognitive order;

---

26 Aulagnier, 2001 [1975]

such de-translation is essentially magnetized by the act that lies in the psyche's originary strata.

Indeed, the non-articulated phrase does not evoke. It is mere presence, it is in action. Now, transference would not be more than banal role-play if it was not essentially led by action. If, then, transference is provoked by the analyst, this nonetheless requires, on the part of the one who provokes, an openness likely to welcome the ensuing effects, however painful or unsettling they might sometimes be. I would thus venture to argue that the analyst who takes full account of the theory of seduction cannot overlook this effect of a counter-hold induced by transference, even though this transference is a response to the enigma of which the analyst is the guardian.

Let us be clear: in my present argument, there is no symmetry in the founding seduction of the analytical situation. Acknowledging the necessity, for the analyst, of a state of passivity-passibility does not imply that the analysand may equally be seen as the issuer of compromised messages. In everyday life, naturally, he is the issuer of compromised messages too but not when his position is the analysand's. In this position, he finds himself re-immersed in the asymmetry of the fundamental anthropological situation. For his part, the analyst must not overlook his own position before the other's sexual enigma, if 'the other' does not refer to 'such-and-such' analysand, or even to analysands in general—as analysands, that is—but to the Other (*Autrui*) following Levinas's use of the term. It is therefore in his own infancy that the analyst is reached, in his *in-fantia*, that is to say his own a-phasia.[27] The latter is brought back into play, put to work again in every analysis: it is the fundamental aphasia against which language emerges, the hollow core of the infantile; it is the inarticulate underside of any spoken word; it is the aphasia the

---

27 I like to point out the fact that a-phasia (Greek etymology) and in-fantia (Latin etymology) equally designate the inability to speak. One could even suggest that, even after his famous 1891 neurological study, Freud never stopped deal-ing with cases of aphasia.

analyst himself seeks—in vain, like everyone else—to remedy and for which the possible antidote is always temporary and flawed, a stutter that arises among words. The analyst can potentially hear this stutter in a new way, when, in the analysand's articulated speech, he manages to catch something of the inarticulate phrase that reaches and affects him in the hollow of transference. A paradoxical thought then seizes the analyst who, against his will, finds himself caught up in that strange entity referred to as 'the analytical chimera' by Michel de M'Uzan (1994). What I will retain here from this chimera is merely the fact that it imposes, within the session, a lived experience of alterity—provided the analyst does not brace himself against the advent of this 'it thinks'. This 'it thinks' has the same modalities as 'it rains': it is a thought devoid of any attributable subject but a usable thought all the same, the outcome of what the analytical apparatus reinstates and foregrounds better than any other human practice, something pertaining to a state of fundamental passivity.[28] The only validation of the relevance and efficacy of this thought will consist in the de-translating effects arising from the subtle balancing act between the seduction set off by the analyst's enigma, on the one hand, and, on the other hand, the analytical holding capacity (*contenance*) and its 'hollow' constituted by the analyst's refusals—refusals that refer back to a state of possibility, passivity more passive than receptivity.

---

28 "It is not the discovery that 'it speaks' or that 'language speaks' that does justice to this passivity. One must show in saying, qua approach, the very deposing or the de-situating of the subject, which nonetheless remains an irreplacable uniqueness…" (Levinas, 1991: 47–48).

The Unpast:
The Actual Unconscious*

To Francine

Opening • 71
  Two Moments of the Actual

A Freudian Project • 78
  Perception, Presence, and the Ego
  The Thing and Its Predicate; Psychic Coating
  The Exclusion of Actual Neuroses… and Their Return
  Hysteria and Soldering

"Aphasia, Infantia" • 90
  Assumption of Intelligibility
  The Case of Dreams
  Double Coating
  Florence
  Actuality and Reality

The Actual and the Sexual • 107
  Theory of Seduction and Ferenczian Chiasm
  The Sexual, the Great Infantile
  The Thing, a Drive-Related Residue

*Translation by Dorothée Bonnigal-Katz, revised by editor and author.

Asymmetrical Couples • 115
    Presenting, (Re-)Presenting, Representing
    On the Extra-Analytical
    Transference (Re-)Presents
    "Lifting-up" the Actual
    The Actual, A Foreign Body

Actuality and Analytic Method • 129
    Crisis of Representation
    Transference, Atemporality, and Actual Time
    An Actual Clock...
    Psychic, Soulical

The Actual, Après-coup, and the Past • 149
    Actuality of Pain and Après-coup
    Characters in Search of a Past
    Beyond Interpretation
    Common Sense and the Untouchable
    Ethics and the Knowledge of the Unconscious

Opening

The Oratory of San Giorgio in Padua features magnificent frescoes by Altichiero da Zevio[1] including an Annunciation[2] distinctive in that it is somewhat difficult to contemplate in broad daylight and is best seen when the weather is overcast or when the lighting inside the chapel is brighter than it is outside. The reason is that lodged in the very middle of the classic scene, between the annunciating angel and the Virgin, is an oculus, a sort of rose window through which, in the daytime, a blinding light usually shines. Visitors wishing to savor this Annunciation—a very beautiful one—must give time for their eyes adjust to the luminous irruption. One might think that this was a constraint imposed on Altichiero which he would have preferred not to have found on the wall where his *affresco* was to be painted, but a wise critic like Daniel Arasse praises this work precisely for the painter's inventiveness and sense of appropriateness in including the oculus in the classic scene of the annunciation.[3] Indeed, what originally appears as a nuisance interfering with contemplation of the work soon, on the contrary, turns out to be an extraordinary deepening of the aesthetic, even the spiritual, experience. The painter found

---

1 Altichiero da Zevio (c. 1330 – c. 1390), whom Vasari calls Aldigeri da Zevio, was a follower of Giotto, who is credited with founding the Veronese school. He worked in Verona and Padua—works by him survive in the church of Sant'Anastasia in Verona and in the basilica of Sant'Antonio and the Oratorio di San Giorgio in Padua.
2 I make a reference to this particular work of art in two chapters of *Quartiers aux rues sans nom* (Scarfone, 2012a).
3 D. Arasse (1999).

a brilliant way to take advantage of the rose window and of its burst of blinding light, by choosing this precise spot for an Annunciation whose rather conventional narrative content is not only intensified, but is transformed: no longer a mere evocation but a lived experience. Altichiero's Annunciation does not only *tell* the classic story; it actually *annunciates, summoning* the spectator, who soon feels seized by this light, without which nothing can be seen, but under whose spell one is but half–blinded.

Interpretations of the Annunciation vary according to whether it is viewed from the religious perspective or abstracted as a representation of the universal experience of being summoned to something that larger than oneself, of being faced with a mystery about which one may never know the last word. There is no need to be a believer to find the presence of something meaningful in the legend,[4] something both unmistakable and hard to put into words, concerning an appeal, a message, addressing a question to, an invitation, a visit, an availability, an offer of hospitality. In short, it refers to anything that breaks the solipsism in which the subject may seem to be locked; an event that presents—and puts us in the presence of—*the other*. The Annunciation is often featured alongside the scene of Adam and Eve's expulsion from the Garden of Eden and scenes of the Passion of Christ. Thus juxtaposed with the joy of bearing and giving birth to the magnificent child, there is the evocation of exile, suffering, and death, For the believer, this is but a prelude to the resurrection and to ultimate salvation, but it can equally well be read as a secular model of the human condition: the announcement of the upcoming advent of His Majesty the Baby, then his arrival overflowing with narcissistic sap; he will be adored and admired, but must gradually learn the limitations imposed by an utterly terrestrial life, degeneration and, eventually, death.

---

4 This story in fact reinstates an earlier biblical scene insofar as the same archangel, Gabriel, forewarned Sarah, Abraham's wife that she would give birth despite her old age.

Opening

Spectators will be able to ponder all this once they have beheld Altichiero's Annunciation, but while their eyes are set on it, they are confronted by a problem of visibility. The light that floods in through the oculus partly blinds them, revealing that they cannot see clearly, that they cannot see everything. It reminds us that we cannot look directly at the sun; that we only have access to what is visible when light is obstructed and comes back to us by a reflection, by a detour. By composing this Annunciation, Arasse calls it a "framing" Annunciation (*Annonciation d'encadrement*), Altichiero not only found an elegant way of integrating into the immense painting the oculus that bores an opening in the chapel's façade, but also, in the same gesture, reminds us that the human spirit does not work in a field of absolute freedom. It is deployed within the constraints of reality; and it is under this pressure that the mind becomes capable of work. This is exactly what Freud means when he posits "resistance" as the necessary condition for all forms of psychic work, resistance that is also the fundamental reason for the resort to an analytic method. A paradoxical method, in fact, whose requirements are all negative: no self-censoring on the side of the *analysand*, no focused attention on the side of the analyst.

In the Oratory of San Giorgio, the oculus was probably just such a resistance for Altichiero, a resistance the painter had to know how to contend with using his own method but which, once worked through, would give the final work a profundity going far beyond what is represented, endowing it with a presence, a status of *presentation*. In saying this, I am not talking about transcendence. All Annunciations evoke the idea of transcendence, of the advent of the infinite within the finite, of the divine within the human. For that purpose, all they need to do is to tell, that is, *to represent*, the familiar story of the tidings brought to Mary. In Altichiero's fresco, what the blinding oculus offers—like any good solution: pictorial, sculptural, musical, or any other—what it offers that is stronger than the narrative, is lived

73

experience, an *actual*[5] presentation. Nevertheless, such a presentation does not offer a direct access to what is there that could be known; on the contrary, it marks the limits of representation. In so doing, it signals that there is something beyond the representable, beyond the understandable, something beyond meaning, an enigmatic depth, an opaque or empty core at the heart of all representation as of all psychic production; something which goes unnoticed most of the time since it is the ego's specific function to attempt a steady return to the same,[6] always to recapture the familiar, scotomizing the alien or, even better, the strangerness (*étrangèreté*).[7]

Two Moments of the Actual

The oculus' presence within the fresco together with its light effect epitomizes the idea I would like to develop of two moments of the actual, two distinct planes on which the actual is manifest. The *first moment* is when the actual appears in an unelaborated form, as a heterogeneous body, a raw obstacle to the work of elaboration; a mass (a hole, in the present case) that resists being taken up into the movement of thought or creativity. The *second moment* is, conversely, when the actual provides a necessary anchoring for lived experience. The actuality of the experience ensures that experience, however subjective it may be, is not free of all ties, is not be destined to be arbitrary. Anchoring in actuality endows experience with the profundity and the density that makes it capable of potentially infinite elaboration while

---

5 The word 'actual' is used here both in the ordinary sense and as in 'actual neurosis', Strachey's translations of Freud's *Aktualneurose*.
6 In one of the notable yet probably unintentional convergences of Levinas's thought with psychoanalysis, the philosopher often relies on the phrase "the same" to refer to the ego. See Levinas (1948).
7 [Editor's note: '*étrangèreté*' is a neologism in French used by both Scarfone and Laplanche. It combines the notions and the connotations of 'strange' (*étrange*) and of stranger/alien (*étrangère*). In UIT editions, we have translated this word with an English neologism "strangerness"; others have chosen "alienness".]

remaining firmly tethered to the flesh of the world. In other words, from the point of view of subjectivity, the actual *in the first sense* is an obstacle, a form of inertia, concealing the potentialities it has to offer. *In the second sense*, the actual as the realization of certain of these potentialities, is what gives representation its gravitational pull.

So initially, insofar as it is not part of the expected scenography of an Annunciation, the *oculus* was "actual" in the first sense of the term. But it became actual in the second sense of the word once the painter found the aesthetic solution to the problem and integrated the *oculus* into his fresco. Thus, the actuality of the oculus has not disappeared, but rather has been elevated to a higher plane, and become what endows the entire piece with a dimension taking it beyond representation—something akin to sublimation.[8] Completed in this way, the work of art does not represent, it *presents*. Such presence, such presentness, does not relate to chronology however; spectators who let themselves be addressed by this presence *of* the work and *in* the work are immersed in an "other time," to borrow Pontalis's phrase which denotes "a time that does not pass."[9]

When one has such an experience, one finds oneself in a state of receptiveness and availability that ordinarily cannot be achieved on demand, but that one can allow for in the most intimate relation to oneself. To approximate this state, one must silence the incessant chatter of the ego as it seeks to name, order, assess, and interpret, instead of *letting something happen*, letting something flow through or even pierce oneself. The vulnerability thus required of spectators is probably related to the sensitivity which, in addition to his talent and technique, the artist requires to find the uncharted path leading to a work that touches the soul. Even with their differences, artist and spectator both find themselves in a position that I will refer to as *infancy* or,

---

[8] I am endorsing here, in my own way, Lacan's definition of sublimation as elevating the object "to the dignity of the Thing" (Lacan, 1959–1960, p. 133).
[9] Pontalis (1994).

inspired by Lyotard,[10] as *infantia*, to stress the fact that, etymologically, the term denotes the incapacity to speak. One might assume that this *infantia* is overcome by language acquisition, but this would overlook the fact that, coextensive with the appearance of language and with the progression toward representation, repression intervenes, imposing limits on both. *Infantia* then merely turns inward and remains buried at the heart of the subject of speech, operating as a disposition for and a liability to new impacts, to traumas, big or small, that will unsettle the soul and reactivate the primal processes, the attendants of an experience that cannot be fully described.

*

An obvious parallel can be drawn between the complementarity of artist and spectators and the one instituted between patient and analyst. The patient supports his request for an analysis with a story and with infantile theories spoken from the locus of an ego that has strived to find a sense of general meaning conjoined with some enjoyment of life, but whose attempts have failed to a greater or lesser extent. But whether he or she comes to analysis with open wounds or, on the contrary, with a firm display of defenses, the analysand will have to be heard by someone who can access a certain kind of sensitivity, of *passibility*,[11] making the analyst able to accommodate the transference of what the channels of speech alone are unable to convey. The transference is a distinctive feature of the "talking cure" that, paradoxically, is the expression in action of whatever eludes the realm of the speakable and can never be fully rendered into words, even by the most advanced interpretations. The analyst's passibility, like the artist's sensitivity, must admittedly be "supported" by a certain

---

10 Lyotard (1991a)
11 I long ago adopted this term, suggested by Jean-François Lyotard, as an alternative to the term passivity. Cf. "*Logos and Technè*, or Telegraphy", in Lyotard (1991 [1988]).

Opening

know-how, but, as Ferenczi was the first to understand (and there lies his genius), the analyst's knowledge must first be based on the lived experience of being in a patient's position.

A Freudian Project

While there is no substitute for the personal experience of analysis, it does not eliminate the necessity, quite the opposite, of reflecting, après-coup, both on the experience and on the practical and metapsychological conditions for its possibility. Theoretical formalization does consist of putting the lessons of experience in canonical terms, but rather of deepening the experience in the direction taken by the analytic treatment itself.[12] For while the analogy between aesthetic experience and the experience of analysis is legitimate, it does not erase the numerous differences between the two situations. One of these differences is that the work of art achieves its goal in the very site of the experience and that, even if the way it marks us may last for a long time, it does not involve a transferential link of the same order as seen in analysis. The analytic experience too is maximal in the site of the experience, in the session, but it would create an untreatable dependence, an entrapment in an interminable analysis, if this experience were not conducted in a way that opens up onto what is outside of the analysis. This requires a "handling" of the transference that makes possible another transference and, by that other transference a path to disengagement, a channeling off the tracks of the hallucinatory mode that in the transference goes hand in glove with the return of repressed. A transference of transference[13] thus imposes itself, the sign of an increased motility of investments, spurring the capacity to

---

12 Scarfone (2011a).
13 Laplanche (1999 [1991])

think, symbolize, and therefore accept separation, absence, and loss. This kind of thinking is not intellectualization but a combining of the effective use of signs with their drive-related source; it is an embodied form of thinking in open contact, via internal channels of communication, with those forms intimately connected with the sensorial, dwelling closest to the sources of the experience.

To assert that a goal of clinical analysis is to facilitate thinking, symbolization, in no way conflicts with the rules that govern the method. Although the analyst suspends representation of goals in each and every session, nevertheless he does not relinquish the overall objective: restoring the subject's capacity to say "I" rather than to remain in one or another of the "freeze-frame" positions that are various versions of his ego.[14] The "I" in question does not have a final version. Following Freud's well-known maxim, the analyst works to foster the emergence of the "I" there "where id was,"[15] although in this process the "I" does not replace the id but arises in the place of a frozen "ego" and emerges endowed with greater flexibility and freer access to the id's modalities. As far as the "I" is concerned, such fluidity is akin to an essential requirement of the art of thinking. The point is to set thinking back in motion, to open up paths. In fact, this is the meaning of the prefix *durch* in *Durcharbeitung*, usually translated as "working through," but which could legitimately be understood as "digging out a pathway."[16]

This fluid kind of thinking on the part of the "I" is like a wind that, in Hannah Arendt's phrase, sweeps away frozen thoughts, the already thought;[17] this involves some destruction, as does any creative work— except that, just as the artist abides by the "rules of art," the

---

14 In a recent book, François Gantheret (2013) has written beautiful pages on the subject.
15 Freud (1932), p. 163.
16 Lyotard, op. cit. In Cinq concepts proposés à la psychanalyse, the sinologist François Jullien suggests the term de-fixation, positing pathway restoration as the basic function of psychoanalysis. Cf. Jullien (2012), p. 131.
17 Arendt (1970).

thinking subject cannot do without a certain knowing-how to think. It would thus be ironic for psychoanalytic thinking to seek fluidity for itself without relating the fluidity to its own rules of art. Without such rules, psychoanalysis would also "freeze on a single frame" because it could not possess a body of knowledge permitting it to draw lessons from analytic experience in a form that is both *transmissible* and *open to critique*. To make psychoanalytic ideas open to critique, we must formulate them in terms with sufficiently precise meaning, which raises the issue of not losing touch with the highly complex sources of the experience, of not sacrificing too much for the sake of the necessary clarity. In other words, there is no necessary contradiction between the analyst's passibility, sensitivity and availability, and, on the other hand, an adequately clear formulation of the lessons of the analytic experience. The tool Freud invented for this purpose is what he called "metapsychology" and later characterized as a witch. Even if he does not use the term in the *Project for a Scientific Psychology* (1895), that text can be regarded as one of Freud's greatest metapsychological texts, as a letter to Fliess from the same period corroborates.[18] Passibility, an openness to the possibility of being reached, is not part of the metapsychological vocabulary, even less so in the *Project*. My hope is to show how that work nonetheless contains the premises of passibility in what Freud refers to as the *perceptual complex*.[19]

Perception, Presence, and the Ego

For Freud, all psychic representation was once perception.[20] Now, perception hosts the first experience of presence, of presentation. In everyday perceptual experience, as in the experience of viewing Altichiero's fresco, the dimension of presentation is gener-

---

18 Freud (1896a).
19 Freud (1895a), especially sections 16, 17 and 18 in part 1 as well as sections 1 and 4 in part 2.
20 Freud (1925b).

ally obscured as a result of the fact that perception entails imitation and empathy which lead back to the known, the familiar. Imitation and empathy create the tie that the perceptual apparatus knots with memory, which is to say with the mnemic images accumulated during earlier perceptions.[21] This is what can be drawn from Freud's observations both in the *Project* and in later texts, which reveal that, in principle, accessing reality would not raise a problem if the apparatus of perception-conscious (pcpt.-cs.) were not linked to a mnemic system, a network of traces that can be invested to the extent that "perceptual signs" are activated and thus the semblance of an actual perception is conjured up, an hallucinatory experience. On the other hand, Freud posits that the perceptual apparatus itself cannot be endowed with memory; if it were, the possibility of perceiving anything new would be jeopardized.[22] However, every perception leaves a mnemic trace, and a certain number of such traces become organized in a "well–facilitated" totality that constitutes the ego. Once structured, this ego, like any structure, sets out to ensure its structural permanence as its first priority; consequently, it welcomes novelty only insofar as it can be accommodated, *assimilated* (that is, made similar) to what is already constituted. This is what I referred to earlier as a "return to the same." Thus novelty, the only thing that can contribute to the subject's evolution, can only arrive as an evolutionary crises, what Michel de M'Uzan calls "identity wobbles," which occur in every individual's history—for example, the long identity crisis epitomized by adolescence—and in every psychoanalytic treatment; so much so, that de M'Uzan considers it a necessary factor for change during the course of the analysis.

---

21 Freud (1895a), *SE* 1 p. 333. One must pay attention here to the meaning of the term *empathy*, however, for if it commonly refers to the familiar, it does not imply the possibility of feeling what the other feels, of "being in communion with"; on the contrary, as Françoise Coblence has shown, empathy must be understood as the process of "capturing at once what is alien to my ego in the other and what is alien to his" (see Coblence 2005, p. 50).
22 Freud (1925a), p. 140.

One of the paradoxes of the ego consists in being the one psychic agency in contact with the external world but only retaining what it can assimilate and so scotomizing the other parts. In this sense, Lacan was right to view the ego as an agent of misrecognition. This in no way makes the ego hateful since, like any living thing, it survives only through its capacity to assimilate what comes its way from without and to adapt the exogenous to its needs. Perception's imitative and empathic aspects are well designed to ensure such vital protection. It is thanks to them that the ego, once in place, does not let the pcpt.-cs. apparatus function on its own. Itself the result of perception (as a network of mnemic traces), the ego directs and focuses attention and, most of the time, perceives only what matches its expectations and fears. When reality imposes an unexpected perception, catching the ego unprepared, there is a risk of trauma. Anxiety as a signal is what must prepare the ego and so ward off the traumatic effect. Yet this signal, this minimal anxiety, is also what activates the filtering process leading to scotomization of the dimension comprising presentation. By imposing a delay in the course of perceptual events, the ego is in sync with the visual apparatus which cannot see without light, but can only see provided it does not look directly at the light. Access to the visible is provided in a roundabout way, via a detour, the introduction of a delay,[23] and with the distortions inherent in any form of repetition. The ego usually does not let itself be caught off guard, and from what it perceives—*a fortiori* from the other, the fellow human being—it only retains the familiar part, what it can understand: in other words whatever bears some resemblance to its own mnemic images.

The Thing and Its Predicate; Psychic Coating

In the *Project* Freud refers to the incomprehensible, inassimilable, inimitable part of the "perceptual complex" as "the thing" (*das*

---

23 Derrida (1978 [1967]).

Ding); this is, Freud states, the part that evades judgment. As for the intelligible part, it is referred to as a "predicate" or "attribute." We are indebted to Lacan for giving prominence to this notion and for gauging its importance in Freud's thought.[24] What I would like to stress at this point is that the perceptual complex described by Freud is more complex than the ego might wish, considering that it prefers to restrict itself to *representation* and experiences anxiety (if only at the low level required for it to be a signal) before a *presentation*. The signal anxiety then mobilizes mechanisms of misknowledge ranging from radical denial to a simple perceptual error (e.g., *lapsus auris*). It's as if it were a case of buying the ego time to mobilize representations so that what presents itself may be endowed with a tolerable "psychic coating." In such a mobilization of representations, the ego naturally ignores the actual part that the motor traces will come to play and that will determine to some extent the form the coating will take, while another part is contingent on elements found close at hand, rather like day residues in dreams.

I am relying on the notion of psychic coating because in my view it is one of the ways Freud revisits, from a clinical perspective, the idea of the attribute covering "the thing." Freud uses this phrase in his presentation of the Dora case, but it figures implicitly in other clinical texts. At stake here is Dora's genital catarrh, the role of which in the young woman's hysterical symptoms Freud is wondering about:

> "In the light of our present knowledge we cannot exclude the possibility of a direct organic influence [of disorders of the genitals]," he writes; "but it is at all events easier to indicate its psychical coating.[25]

This of course is a brief, rather undeveloped mention, a phrase coined as if in passing, but it replicates the model of the "perceptual

---

24 Lacan (1959–1960).
25 Freud (1905b), SE VII, p. 84.

complex" described by Freud in the *Project*. It evokes a "thing" of which ultimately we know nothing but which, once endowed with a psychic coating, that is, with describable attributes, a predicate, will present a comprehensible appearance, an analyzable one. More specifically, the analysis would elicit, among other results, a redrawing of the sinuous links between the "coating" and the actual anchoring. The crux of the matter in all this lies neither in the coating nor in the anchoring but in the *work*, possible or not, between the two, as Freud envisioned with regard to the manifest and latent content of dreams.

The Exclusion of Actual Neuroses… and their Return

If we look closely, the whole Freudian project seems to develop under the rubric of this partition of perception between thing and predicate. One could even argue that the *Project* itself, which includes that conception of the perceived, having been hidden by its author does not merely describe this insurmountable division but actually *exemplifies* it. Such is the actuality of the *Project*! This text marks Freud's transition from neurology to psychology and it seems to have shown Freud that the attempt to reduce psychology to neurology leaves an irreducible residue and thus prevented Freud from making the relation between the neurobiological and the psychic comprehensible. It is as if the very text that denotes the irreparable hiatus between brain and psyche had to be buried, unknown. Throughout his life Freud hoped that this hiatus would, one day, be bridged, but that until then it was necessary to a resort to some form of psychic coating.

Around the same period, between 1894 and 1896, Freud thus began to develop a method that he would first refer to by using a term in French: "*psycho-analyse;*" a method whose application he restricted exclusively to neuropsychoses (or psychoneuroses) of defense, explicitly excluding the "actual neuroses" which, at the time, numbered two: neurasthenia and anxiety neurosis.[26] Their banishment was irre-

---

[26] Freud later added hypochondria.

vocable; many years later Freud retained the original distinction. In *Introductory Lectures on Psycho-Analysis* of 1915-1917 he writes:

> The problems of the 'actual' neuroses, whose symptoms are probably generated by direct toxic damage, offer psycho-analysis no points of attack. It can do little towards throwing light on them and must leave the task to biologico-medical research.[27]

It is thus exclusion of the actual neuroses, claimed to arise from organic processes, that unveils the clinical domain of psychoanalysis. At this stage of conceptualization, of the two "moments" of the actual that I introduced at the beginning of this work, one could say that the actual neuroses instantiate the first moment, comparable to the oculus before the painter found a function for it in the fresco of the Annunciation. For the actual neuroses this refers to the actual before its reintegration in the context of psychoanalysis. Such reintegration is inevitable: Freud is well aware that what is excluded is not thereby abolished, but returns. This return of what is excluded is best seen in the return of the repressed within the domain of neuroses of defense, but Freud recognizes that it also occurs in the actual neuroses, or at least to a feature which is specific to them. In fact, from the beginning Freud is aware that there are no neuroses which are purely actual or purely neuroses of defense. Therefore, if actual neuroses as distinct clinical entities are not accessible to the method of psychoanalysis, they do not disappear from the clinical field nor from the theoretical horizon of psychoanalysis. Thus Freud states, as early as 1896:

> The actual causes which produce neurasthenia and anxiety neurosis often at the same time play the part of exciting causes of the neuroses of defense; on the other hand, the specific causes of a defense-neurosis—the traumas of childhood—can at the same time lay the

---

27 Freud (1917), SE XVI, p. 389.

foundation for a later development of neurasthenia. Finally, it not infrequently happens, too, that neurasthenia or anxiety neurosis is maintained, not by actual sexual noxae, but, instead, by the persisting effect of a memory of childhood traumas.[28]

We have ask what permits such transitivity between the two forms of neurosis that are originally posited as foreign to each other. In any case, let us note that Freud seems to find his bearings, both clinically and theoretically, using the relation that structures the perceptual complex: a nucleus of actual neurosis, opaque to any analysis, is located at the heart of the analyzable psychoneurosis—as a whole, it has the form of the *thing* wrapped in its attributes.

Hysteria and Soldering

As early as his theoretical chapter[29] in *Studies on Hysteria*, Freud describes a structure comparable to the structure in the *Project*: the organization of hysteria is conceived of as a series of themes "stratified concentrically round the pathogenic nucleus."[30] Resistance increases as one approaches this nucleus, the threads of association break off, leading Freud to write that "it is quite hopeless to try to penetrate directly to the nucleus of the pathogenic organization."[31] Even if this nucleus is not as impenetrable as the *thing*, Freud nonetheless says that "the interior layers [surrounding the nucleus] of the pathogenic organization are increasingly alien to the ego"[32] which ends up giving them a comparable strangerness.[33] In the *Introductory Lectures*, Freud gives the same account adding that the actual neuro-

---

28 Freud (1896b), *SE* III, p. 168 (translation modified).
29 [Entitled "The Psychotherapy of Hysteria"]
30 Freud (1893), *SE* II, p. 289
31 Ibid. p. 292
32 *Op. cit.*, p. 290.
33 See page 74 footnote 7

ses (by then comprising three forms: neurasthenia, anxiety neurosis, and hypochondria) "occur occasionally in their pure form; most often, however, they are intermixed with each other and with a psychoneurotic disorder."[34] This, he says, must not prompt us to abandon their separation, just as we distinguish the various minerals that form a rock. Further on in the *Introductory Lectures*, Freud returns to the idea he sketched out in 1905 regarding Dora:

> A noteworthy relation between the symptoms of the 'actual' neuroses and of the psychoneuroses makes a further important contribution to our knowledge of the formation of symptoms in the latter. For a symptom of an 'actual' neurosis is often the *nucleus* and *first stage* of a psychoneurotic symptom.[35]

Caution leads him to add that a nucleus of actual neurosis is not found in all psychoneurotic symptoms, but other passages allow us to infer that the psychoneurotic dimension regularly locks onto an actual factor, covering it with a "psychical coating." It is in this way that Freud says of the meaning of Dora's hysterical symptom:

> The hysterical symptom does not carry this meaning with it, but the meaning is lent to it, *soldered* to it, as it were; and in every instance the meaning can be a different one, according to the nature of the suppressed thoughts which are struggling for expression.[36]

The notion of *soldering* should be underlined; in some of Freud's texts it indicates the kind of separation—established since the *Project*—between *thing* and *predicate*. In fact, the junction that soldering creates is not a form of unification nor the harmonious integration of the two elements soldered together. Moreover, it is

---

34 Freud (1917), *SE* XVI, p. 390.
35 *Op. cit.* p. 390 (italics mine).
36 Freud (1905 [1901]), SE VII, pp. 40–41, italics mine.

reminiscent of the notion, which comes much later, of the mixture or intrication of the life and death drives, for which no true merger is possible. Freud also invokes "soldering" with reference to anxiety in dreams,[37] in the relation between the sexual fantasy and the masturbatory act,[38] and in his account of the formation of Hans's horse phobia.[39] In each instance, the relation between the elements soldered together is similar. Variable representations—scenes in a dream, fantasies, hysterical symptoms, witnesses to the diversity of psychic productions—are soldered to a core which is opaque and *constant* (excitation, irritation, anxiety) that they cover up – they provide a psychic coating. The psychic coating mentioned in the Dora case occurs following the paradigm of the perceptual complex for a fellow human being, but showing even more clearly the role played by the work of remembering. In fact, let us recall that in the *Project* the perceptual complex

> falls apart into two components, of which one makes an impression by its constant structure and stays together as a *thing*, while the other can be *understood* by the *work of remembering* (*Erinnerungsarbeit*)—that is, can be traced back to information from [the subject's] own body. This dissection of a perceptual complex is described as *cognizing* (*erkennen*) it; it involves a *judgement* and when this last aim has been attained it comes to an end.[40]

---

[37] Freud (1900), *SE* IV, p. 462.
[38] Freud (1908), *SE* IX, p. 161.
[39] Laplanche (1980), p. 114.
[40] Freud (1895), *SE* I, p. 331. Italics are Freud's, except for the phrase "the work of remembering." [Translator's note: Translation modified: in the *Standard Edition*, the German term *Erinnerungsarbeit* is translated as "the activity of memory" in the *Project*, but in "Remembering, Repeating and Working-Through" (1914) it is translated as "the work of remembering" (SE XII, p. 153). In keeping with the consistent use of the term *"remémoration"* in French, I have modified the English translation of the Project and opted for the phrase "the work of remembering" throughout.

Note that while the general model is the same, the construction of the symptom, hysterical soldering, does not reduce to the act of perception; consequently, the psychic coating presupposes more complex mechanisms than the automatic partition that occurs within the perceptual complex. Nevertheless, the parallel between the *thing/predicate* pair and the *actual/psychoneurotic* pair remains relevant.

"Aphasia, Infantia"

The paradigm of the perceptual complex is borne out in yet another aspect of Freud's thinking during this prolific period. Abandoning neurological research, Freud makes a leap which takes him from organic aphasia[41] to another difficulty in speaking. The new domain, losing the Greek designation of *a-phasia*, takes as its name its exact Latin translation: *in-fantia*.[42] From that time onward, childhood, or rather *infancy*, which occupies a central place in psychoanalysis, presents an intelligible aspect to the extent that its repressed, unspeakable residues can be given a "psychic coating" by the work of remembering. From the beginning of psychoanalysis, the work of remembering (*Erinnerungsarbeit*)—the notion appearing in the quote at the end of the previous section—suggests not so much the process of retrieving memories as the formation or the reformation of the psychic.[43] Rather than simply remembering, evoking, or "recalling," the "work of remembering" involved in understanding the attributes of the perceptual complex can, in my view, be conceived as a "remembering of oneself to oneself." The subject who perceives must draw on his own mnemic images to be able to understand the other and, especially, must resort to *motor* images, the only images which enable the passing of an effective judgment on what is being observed in

---

41 Freud (1891).
42 The Latin *infans* literally means "who cannot speak."
43 With some adjustments, I am relying on Jean Imbeault's notion of recomposition (1997). See also Scarfone (2007) and the chapter "Repetition: Between presence and meaning" in this book.

the human other.⁴⁴ Thus the work of remembering is inscribed in a relation to the other that is also a relation to the self, inasmuch as one "relates to" or "reports to" oneself after having been disorientated by the incompletely graspable perception of the human other. This provides a basis from which to resume our reflection on the work of the analytic session, as I will do later.

The exclusion of actual neuroses, the metapsychological formulations of the *Project*, and the discovery of a method of dream interpretation all occur during the same short period between 1894 and 1896. At the same time, the gradual development of the analytic method is under way, following Freud's rejection of hypnosis, suggestion, and Breuer's cathartic method. If there was a generative period in Freud's thinking, this was it! Freud's creativity is dramatically impressive but if necessity is the mother of invention then this applies to Freud's inventiveness as well: it logically ensues from the acknowledgment of a limit, of an unbridgeable gap inscribed within the world of human perception. From this it follows that the psychoanalytic *infantia*, which takes the torch from neurological aphasia, is not an *infantia* such as the word suggests at first sight; it is not simply that age of life before the mastery of language. The impossibility of understanding the whole of the *Nebenmensch* (the fellow human being) is a structural fact about the relation established between two beings, whatever their age or facility with language. In this sense, everyone who encounters another human being is partly an *infans*. Something in the perception of our fellow humans always escapes our grasp, even if the perceiving subject seems to possess the means by which to understand and imitate the other. We must accept and take into account this blockage, or else the project of knowing the other must turn into an abusive interpretation.⁴⁵

What ensues is an idea that appears astonishing at first sight.

---

44 Leclaire and Scarfone (2000); Laurence Kahn (2012).
45 "Secondary violence" in Piera Castoriadis-Aulagnier's view (1975).

Psychoanalysis—which seems to be based on the assumption that human doings, even the most absurd, are intelligible—is only made possible by the fact that, when all is said and done, humans *do not understand one another*.[46] Consequently, if the goal of psychoanalysis were to make human behavior and motivation completely *transparent*, psychoanalysis would be ethically monstrous. What I am positing is the opposite: an *opaque* nucleus, the *actual* core of the self and the other, is a foundational and unsurmountable fact, opening the very possibility of a psychoanalysis *at the service* of those who suffer, and not an instrument of power or mastery over them. The analyst does not seek to eradicate this opaque core, which in any case would be impossible, but to ensure it a psychic covering. The hermeneutic conceptions of contemporary psychoanalysis, however well-intentioned they may be in their attempt to release meaning, must know how to take account of this aspect of the clinical reality, otherwise they run the serious risk of an authoritarian drift, no matter how lenient their formulations, or else they are doomed to remain within the sphere of the familiar, circumventing the strangeness of the unconscious.

Assumption of Intelligibility

The initial exclusion of the actual neuroses might seem to indicate that Freud, well aware of the split between thing and predicate, is making a choice in favor of the second term, which is to say a choice on the side of hermeneutic intelligibility. An entire dimension of his interpretive deciphering suggests that Freud—admittedly for a relatively short time—prefers to work on the side most likely to shed light, to find a meaning, and so to escape the aphasia or *infantia* under which the enigma of hysteria is submerged. Thus the escape is on the side of the decodable, of what can be "guessed" at in the ingenious constructions that are the psychoneuroses. Probably swept along by the powerful wave of his method for interpreting dreams, Freud

---

46 André et al. (2012).

seems to pay most attention to what is interpretable, to the side of the attributes, to the predicate—in short to what in the end can be listed under the heading of the *psychic* in so far as the psychic contrasts with what remains *actual*, such as the neuroses of the that name.

I believe, however, that Freud's choice is only apparent. As Jean Laplanche stresses in more than one place, what characterizes Freud's investigations is fidelity to his object.[47] He may often stray, but he never loses sight of what fundamentally inspires and guides his work: the unconscious, the *unconscious thing*. So, even if at times his attention momentarily seems more focused on the intelligible side than on the side of *"thingness,"* it is never for long that he leaves the *unconscious thing* outside the scope of his research. In the end, the *thing* that seems neglected always returns. An obvious parallel can be drawn between, on the one hand, the temporary neglect and the return of the *thing*, and on the other hand, the initial exclusion of the actual neuroses followed by their later reinsertion in more comprehensive psychoanalytic formulations. Without conflating the two notions, it seems to me that the actual neuroses and the *thing* have in common an essential phenomenon, which is precisely their… *actuality*. As I have shown, early on Freud finds what is actual in the actual neuroses at the very heart of the psychoneuroses. It should come as no surprise, that the *thing*, seemingly neglected while Freud was intent on solving the enigmas of dreams and psychoneuroses by the interpretive method, should also make an unexpected return in the actuality of this clinical work.

The Case of Dreams

Therefore, let us linger on the forms in which "thingness" returned in the heart of the psychic, notably in *The Interpretation of Dreams*. While this great book of 1900 arouses interest primarily because it offers a method of *elucidation* of these enigmatic nocturnal

---

47 Laplanche (2015[1993]).

events, we know all that Freud inferred about the general functioning of the apparatus that produces them and especially about the significance of the hallucinations. The book does not consider dreams only in terms of their content, manifest or latent, but also in relation to the *processes* that underlie them. The attention given to primary processes, which dreams illustrate better than any other psychic production, brings to light the underlying mechanisms of displacement and condensation whose importance is not only revealing what constitutes the dream-work, but also indicate the center around which the hallucinatory experience of the dream gravitates.

That fact that displacement and condensation are aspects of the dream work implies that dreams make use of signs other than verbal ones. Here we should remember the semiotic triad developed at the same time, on the other side of the Atlantic, by Charles Sanders Peirce.[48] Alongside the conventional signs of verbal language—the only signs for which Peirce uses the term *symbols*—he identifies two other types of signs: *indexes*, denoting a relation of causality or contiguity between the sign and the designated thing, and *icons*, signs bearing a graphic resemblance to the designated thing. Note how indexes and icons lend themselves, respectively, to the mechanism of displacement (association via contiguity; indexical relation) and condensation (association via resemblance; iconic relation).[49] The indexical and iconic values of the signs handled by primary processes distinguish them from verbal signs, in that indexes and icons maintain a more direct connection with sensation; thus they are closer to the materiality and form of what they designate than are abstract, purely conventional words. A drawing of a cloud (an iconic sign) retains something of what it denotes so that, regardless of what language is spoken, everyone is able to identify in it the reference to the designated thing, whereas the verbal sign greatly varies from one lan-

---

48 Peirce (1894).
49 Scarfone (2013).

"Aphasia, Infantia"

guage to the next (*cloud, nuage, molnet, Wolke*, etc.) with no relation to the sensory dimension. This accords with the idea that primary processes which are at work in the production of hallucinatory experience tend toward the identity of perception. However, this identity is never complete. Given the displacements and the condensations involved, the other characteristic of indexical and iconic signs is a great *plasticity*. Thus dreams must *transform* what they seek to represent as an identity. This is likely what leads Freud, at the end of a rich series of observations, to conclude chapter VI of *The Interpretation of Dreams*, with this rather categorical assertion:

> [The dream-work] does not think, calculate or judge in any way at all; it restricts itself to giving things a new form. [...] The thoughts have to be reproduced exclusively or predominantly in the material of visual and acoustic memory-traces, and this necessity imposes upon the dream-work *considerations of presentability* which it meets by carrying out fresh displacements."[50]

As presentability requires new displacements, taking presentability into consideration means that dreams cannot re-present without distortion. It also means that there will always be an unrepresented and, ultimately, an unrepresentable residue. This is one of the possible meanings of a point Freud makes twice in the same work: that every dream has a *navel*, a point that is impervious to analysis and by which the dream is connected to "the unknown."[51]

Freud notices that something in the dream resists understanding and "at that point there is a tangle of dream-thoughts which

---

50 Freud (1900), SE IV, p. 507. [Tr. Strachey's translation of *Darstellbarkeit* is "representability"; I have opted for "presentability," following Laplanche and his team of translators, for whom *Darstellung* is better rendered as *"presentation,"* the objective mode. "Representation," which is more subjective, is a more appropriate translation for *Vorstellung*.]
51 *Op. cit.*, p. 111 note 1 and p. 525.

cannot be unravelled and which *moreover adds nothing to our knowledge of the content of the dream.*"⁵² At first sight this seems a truism: if nothing can be said about the thoughts the navel is made up of, these thoughts in no way shed any light for us on the content of the dream. But I believe that the phrase "adds nothing" is key, but that Strachey's translation is insufficient here: the sentence in German reads "*keine weiteren Beiträge geliefert hat*"⁵³ which literally means "makes no *further* contribution." Considering what Freud states elsewhere regarding the psychic coating of the organic nucleus in hysteria or regarding the "soldering" of anxiety to a dream content or a phobic object to which the anxiety in question does not necessarily correspond, it seems fair to think that if the obscure spot of the dream, its navel, makes no *further* contribution it is because it has made its *full* contribution as the solid core of "presence" that haunts the dream's content.

On the one hand, this core, this navel, is the "thingness" of the content that exerts the force of attraction⁵⁴ or gravitational pull according to which the latent dream–thoughts are organized. On the other hand, those dream–thoughts are usually transposed into a more or less random manifest content (which depends largely on the day residue or on older scenes), which is connected to the dream thoughts through some detail that in itself is insignificant. This then raises the question of what permits dream processes to form and maintain such links, however insubstantial, between latent thoughts and dream–images. The answer, of course, is that the psychic apparatus seeks to reproduce the coordinates of the experience of satisfaction in a hallucinatory mode. What is involved, as I have already mentioned, is a tendency toward an identity of perception. Yet, as I also pointed out, dreams cannot attain such identity, cannot reproduce the sensory coordinates of the experience identically. Relying on the general model implicit in the *Project*, we can say that the *thing* persists,

---

52 *Op. cit.* p. 525 (italics mine).
53 *GW*, vol. II-III, p. 530.
54 Pontalis (1990), *La force d'attraction*, Paris, Le Seuil, Bibliothèque du XXe Siècle.

so that the any dream images can attach themselves to the dream-thoughts by virtue of the force of attraction of that umbilical *thing*. In this phrase, "force of attraction" is not only a metaphor. Thoughts and images are summoned because one cannot confront the *thing* for very long without trying to coat it psychically. The work of covering up[55] what presents itself is not decorative. It is a process of binding that, in *Beyond the Pleasure Principle*, Freud considers to be the essential function of the psychic apparatus and that ultimately he ascribes to dreams themselves:[56] binding the quantities of excitation imposed by what presents itself and, in this way, preventing anxiety, or even fright. The absence of representation is intolerable and so an apparatus in good working order is quick to construct, to cobble up any old representation, provided it results in at least a semblance of meaning. If the binding is thwarted by the quantity of excitation or by lack of preparation, the situation deteriorates, damaging the psychic apparatus itself, which then must resort to discharge as its only solution, either toward the outside which is action, or toward the interior of the body which is somatization—all under the aegis of the repetition compulsion. The actual, thingness, therefore operates in the literal sense of being an obstacle, a blockage, an impasse.

Double Coating

If, as I am inclined to think, the thing/predicate relation constitutes a paradigm for the organization and the dynamics of the unconscious, in the case of dreams the mechanism gets more complex. In fact, as we have begun to see, the coating of the *thing* is doubled. On the one hand, it is wrapped up in the inextricable network of dream-thoughts, this "tangle" within which, Freud writes,

---

55 Interestingly, the French term recouvrement, which is used in the original, refers to a process of *covering up* as well as a process of *recovery* (recapturing), thus evoking the work of remembering.
56 Freud (1920), pp. 32–33.

"at some point where this meshwork is particularly close . . . the dream-wish grows up, like a mushroom from its mycelium."[57] In dreaming, as we know, a non-verbal mode of expression takes over. If, following our model, dream-thoughts occupy the place where the predicate gravitates around the *thing*, these dream-thoughts must, in turn, be re-coated with dream-*images*. One must factor in this division of the means of expression, or else one runs the risk of remaining trapped in a purely cognitive view of the "perceptual complex" that, up to this point, has served as our guide. It is no coincidence that *The Interpretation of Dreams*, especially chapter VII, should take up the torch from the *Project* which Freud had scrapped.[58] Primary processes are not only cognitive, but also carry the economic energy of libidinal investment. Thus, thoughts do not operate simply as predicates, rather they are invested, then disinvested, distorted by repression, subjected to the displacement of their libidinal charges; in their turn, they make up a sort of nucleus around which the dream-images gravitate. The appearance of another means of expression, of a language specific to dreams, is certainly required by the state of sleep but in fact this state merely *reveals* the existence of a psychic stratum where *at every moment* "it thinks" in images, in the form of scenes: this is the stratum of fantasy, of a specific activity of thought that stages repressed thoughts (Aulagnier); thoughts, let us not forget, that secondary repression has de-symbolized, designified and thus made them similar, though not identical, to the *thing*.

A close study of dreams teaches us, as Laurence Kahn has emphasized, that while these images are thoughts *presented* as images, nevertheless they are not images *of* thoughts.[59] In other words, dream processes do not *translate* thoughts into images as one would when translating a sign for a sign, a verbal language into an iconic language.

---

57 Freud (1900), op. cit., p. 525.
58 See Green (1972).
59 Kahn (2012), p. 48.

This is a decisive point which distinguishes Freud's approach from any form of cognitivism: in dreams, signs as theorized by Peirce do not replace one another following a linear logic of translation (an image for a word); this logic is subverted by the force of attraction of the *thing* that the dream-wish seeks in vain to recapture in the hallucinatory experience. The dream, Freud reminds us, does not think; therefore it does not translate but merely *transforms* thoughts into images. How? By *soldering* the images to a network of thoughts. A "do-it-yourself" presentation is cobbled together drawing on what happens to be available for use as a day residue, facilitated by the freedom of movement conferred by the primary processes. All that is required of the images that contribute to the construction of the dream is that they lend themselves to a possibility of expression, of presentation: a demand for presentability rather than figurability.[60] This implies that by gravitating around the *thing*, the thoughts transformed into images are not a representation whose form is dictated by the *thing* (in the sense of being a figurative version of it); rather, they are a *manifestation* of its presence.

While the thing/predicate model applies to dream-thoughts and dream–images, the issue of affects remains to be addressed. On this subject, Kahn states that "the dream–work brings not only the content but also the affective tone of thoughts to 'the level of the indifferent.'"[61] Such work is possible insofar as affects, both pleasant and unpleasant, can in their unpleasant form come down to a feeling of tension. Since tension does not seem "to refer to any painful thought—and that is the theoretical contribution of the actual neuro-

---

60 I concur with Kahn's position on this matter who also insists on using "presentability" rather than figurability, the latter expression being promoted by the Botellas (2005).[Tr. The term 'figurability' in relation to dreams was first used by Mahoney in 1975 and not again until Castoriadis' 1992 paper. See Mahony (1975). "The Interpretation of Dreams, Semiology, and Chomskian Linguistics—A Radical Critique." Psychoanal. St. Child, 30:221-24 and Castoriadis (1992). "Logic, Imagination, Reflection" Amer. Imago, 49:3-33 1]
61 *Op. cit.*, p. 87.

ses—affects are [...] apprehended as pure quantity.... The affect thus becomes the index of excitation itself."[62]

Let us stress that this duality of affects is yet another example of the partition between a part which is describable, if only with the rudimentary qualifiers of pleasure and unpleasure, and a nucleus in close proximity to "pure quantity," an *index of excitation*. The notion of an index locates us within the orbit around an opaque core, itself unrepresentable—but whose trace can be soldered to any expressive form—compatible with a satisfaction, however minimal, and able to end up as a representation, which is to say, able in some fashion to be *thought*.

Before getting to there, however, I must disentangle the series of transfers that have occurred between the quality-affect and the dream-images, the successive displacements, condensations, and transpositions that insert themselves between dreams and diurnal thoughts: operations carrying a quantity that is not always easy to guess, unless by work comparable to *stripping off* of the layer of substitute representations. With any luck, stripping off the layer may uncover a stratum where the "presentation" becomes active in the transference, where the experience is lived in the actual mode, *in praesentia*, before the psyche is able to recapture the traces left by the work of repression and hold onto them in an attempt to carry out a re-elaboration. The actual that operates in the lived experience of transference may then form a bridge between two subjectivities.

Florence

Florence, a young woman in her thirties, arrives at her session one day with her mind wholly occupied with trying to remember the name of a famous pianist, "*Claudio* something," whose exceptionally gentle playing she loved. All she could remember was the name Abbau, but she knew that was not it. Abbau led her to Abbado, but

---

62 *Op. cit.*, p. 91.

"Aphasia, Infantia"

that was a conductor. Finally, the name Claudio Arrau emerged. She wondered (and so did I) what might have blocked her access to this name, and why all those detours.

At first, not knowing what to think and probably influenced by the model of the forgotten name Signorelli,[63] I listed all the names that successively came up on a piece of paper:

ABBAU

ABBADO

ARRAU

I then realized—and later pointed it out to Florence without drawing any conclusion—that by superimposing the three names and removing the elements they had in common, namely, A, B, and U,

~~ABBAU~~

~~ABBADO~~

~~ARRAU~~

we were left with DO (a musical note and the first syllable of my name) and RR, which I heard as a growling sound that might be made by a voracious animal. This baffled Florence. It so happened that she had previously had had a dream she had not yet mentioned in which a Great Dane attacked two men and devoured them. In the dream, Florence said of one of them: "That'll teach him to play psychoanalyst!" This dream, which undoubtedly expressed, to say the least, an affective impulse, turned out to be the result of a series of complex permutations in the play of representations and affects. The Great Dane led Florence's associations and without thinking she said: "Last week, I stuffed my face with nuts." I stressed the word "nuts" (*noix* in French), which is embedded in the French name for the breed

---

63 Freud (1898).

Great Dane: *Danois* = Dane. This opened up an important piece of Florence's oedipal history. Along with chocolate, nuts were among the few things that Florence's mother kept in a locked drawer in the kitchen. She kept them exclusively for her husband, Florence's father. Such a seemingly banal fact took on great meaning when Florence understood the ludicrous means of seduction her mother used with her husband, who was a womanizer, as my patient now knew. The stash of nuts and chocolate was meant to support, as best she could, the mother's somewhat precarious position on the oedipal scene, a position further imperiled by an incestuous climate in which the father had the audacity to become the lover of his daughter's best friend! Moreover, the "father's nuts" held captive in "the maternal drawer" served as a primal scene.

One thing I did not tell Florence deserves to be mentioned here, because it was what led me to think of the RR as a growl: the sound ABBAU, the first one to come to her mind, evoked in me, before I knew anything about the Great Dane in her dream, a common but very significant word in my childhood. "*U'bau-bau*" was in fact the name for the wolf used by adults when telling children scary stories. I first thought that this association was mine alone, and that the proximity of this wolf to the voracious dog in the dream was a mere coincidence, but coming back to this previously presented episode,[64] I see things differently. Wasn't my association more importantly related to the climate of orality that had gradually built up during Florence's sessions and in which we were both steeped without truly realizing it. It appeared as if the images, like that of the Great Dane, had arisen from verbal bridges specific to Florence's history (the nuts) and had found some echo in me via that other verbal bridge that appeared within her slips of the tongue, acts of devouring words themselves. As pointed out by one of my colleagues,[65] DO and RR, the results of

---

64 See Scarfone (2006) this volume chapter 1.
65 The colleague in question is Martin Gauthier.

the decomposition of the three names, present themselves as scraps, as the remains of a process of devouring applied, this time, to representations, certainly verbal but treated as things.

From an unpleasant affective charge, which was actual, the dream–work led to a dream experience which was held, temporarily, outside of consciousness, then transferred onto preconscious representations, in search of a substitute that would be its antidote (the gentleness of Arrau's piano playing as opposed to cannibalistic violence), clouding the clues, disrupting the memory and the verbal signifiers in a way similar to the very act whose presentation is being kept at bay. A sinuous progression, a quest in the course of which Florence's successive slips of the tongue allowed an outline to appear in reverse order. This outline has become visible through the mediation of the sensory trace (RR, indexical sign) hidden in the proper name (verbal sign) of the beloved pianist. Because the analysis had been conducted without a specific aim, the trace of the thing ultimately *presented itself*, and was met with a strong acknowledgment on Florence's part. What came back to her then was not only the memory, but the lived, hallucinatory sensation of the dog in the dream, a dog whose wild voraciousness emerged as an *actual experience* that gripped the patient and, for a moment, terrified her. The dog thus does not belong to the sphere of representation. On the contrary, it is a vibrant, expressive form, inscribed in the sound material that seeped in through the double slip: a threatening growl bursting forth in the very place where the point was to evoke a pianist with an "exceptionally gentle" touch. The voraciousness suggested by the indexical sign RR was certainly reinforced by the Abbau/U'bau-bau assonance, but one can equally well assume that the childish signifier of the wolf was, conversely, invoked in me by RR, guided as I was by the series of names suggested by Florence.

Through other dreams we were led to the anorexia of Florence's adolescence, as well as to the illness that almost made her lose all her teeth around the time her mother killed herself. All these stories were "known," but like the Great Dane, their words and sentences had to become embodied[66] in the actuality of transference in order at last to be spoken, an act of remembering defined by Freud as "reproduction in the psychical field,"[67] as opposed to what tends to present itself in a hallucinatory mode or as acted-out repetition.

Actuality and Reality

The dream experience imposes itself, presents itself, without asking the dreamer's permission. The dream is a visitor coming from another place, created in "another scene." It sets the ego aside. This has been said often enough that I need not go over it. Moreover, Freud says the same thing about our entire relation to the perceived world. He puts it in a nutshell while discussing the "oceanic feeling": "We cannot fall out of this world."[68] Having referred to that feeling as an "intellectual perception," he soon developed an interest in it, positing the notion of an "all-embracing ... primary ego-feeling," an ego that "includes everything" and from which we must take away the elements that

> evade him from time to time—among them, what he desires most of all, his mother's breast—and only reappear as a result of his screaming for help. In this way there is for the first time set over against the ego an 'object', in the form of something which exists 'outside' and which is only forced to appear by a special action.[69]

The object world thus presents itself by *setting itself in opposition*. As to why we perceive, why the pcpt.-cs, apparatus is periodically

---

66 Gantheret (1998).
67 Freud (1914a), *SE* XII, p. 152.
68 Freud (1930), *SE* XXI, p. 65.
69 *Op. cit.*, p. 67.

invested, why it occasionally "savors" the surrounding world, Freud's dicta on this subject are well known. For example, in a much commented on passage from "On Negation," he says that the point is to check whether what is represented inside still exists outside. This can be read as reprising a Darwinian principle of survival, as well as an economic principle: avoid triggering an action for which the sought-after object does not exist. In this regard, as we have seen, the binding of the pcpt.-cs. apparatus and the memory systems may jeopardize the process: the intensity with which a trace is invested can, at least in principle, endow it with as much of an indication of reality as an object in the external world. The issue then is to inhibit the hallucinatory tendency through a "correct use of perception signs." This is what is generally referred to as reality testing.

In a detailed study of this question, Marie Leclaire and I come to distinguish between reality testing and actuality testing.[70] We realized that in relation to what excites the perceptual apparatus, internally as well as externally, the latter operates in two distinct stages, however close together they might be: there is an *actuality effect*, which applies to external perception as well as to the intense reactivation of mnemic images (past perceptions). At this level, external perception and hallucination are not clearly distinct. What elicits the distinction is *actuality testing*, which stems from the ego's inhibiting function. By virtue of its mere presence, the ego can inhibit the "signs of actuality" coming from internal excitation and thus pave the way toward reality testing.[71] What completes the process in reality testing is the activation of a particular category of mnemic images: *motor* images or traces, which precisely coincide with the ones invoked by Freud when accounting for the "imitation-value" and "sympathy-value" of a perception:

---

70 Leclaire and Scarfone (2000). René Roussillon (1991) used the phrase *actuality testing* but without providing a definition for it or addressing its metapsychological status.
71 Leclaire and Scarfone, *op. cit.*, pp. 902–905

> While one is perceiving the perception, one copies the movement oneself—that is, one innervates so strongly the motor image of one's own which is aroused towards coinciding [with the perception], that the movement is carried out.[72]

The arousal of motor images does not always lead to a manifest muscular action as the ego can inhibit its subsequent development secondarily, but it activates an essential function, that of *judging*, in relation to the fact of *identifying*.[73] Leclaire and I thus concluded that the hallucination exercises its power only when the activation of motor images fails to occur. When motor images do not come together with the signs of perception, the forceful cathexis of other mnemic traces can take the place of a perception. In a context in which the psyche is passive, the hallucinatory mode prevails and imposes itself as an act; this pertains to the actual. Indeed, when reality testing fails, when the ego's presence is not adept at inhibiting the signs of actuality coming from internal sources, and when motor traces in addition remain dormant, then all is actual.

Here an interesting corollary seems to emerge: if the motor traces are required for reality testing to occur and to establish the final distinction between perception and representation, we must infer, given that motor traces are intimately linked to the body, that motor traces and the body in fact elicit the work of remembering instead of the hallucination. As we have seen, remembering consists less in evoking memories than in "remembering of oneself to oneself," and this process of remembering implies a reference to one's motor experience. Yet it is clear that this is also what underlies the distinction between fully psychic representation and acted-out repetition and/or hallucination. It is thus a fact that "psyche is bodily" (Coblence). I would go even further: psyche is motor, it is the animation of the soul itself (see below).

---

72 Freud, (1950 [1895a]), *SE* I, p. 333. Brackets in the original.
73 *Op. cit.*, pp. 332–335.

The Actual and the Sexual

While it may be true that in his work with hysterics, Freud shifts the emphasis onto the side of meaning at the expense of the side of the *thing*, nonetheless he carries out a major reversal in the clinical approach to those suffering beings: seeking a meaning in their symptoms, he starts listening to them rather than making a spectacle of them as did Charcot. Freud's bet on the intelligibility of the psychoneuroses should not be undervalued, without that intelligibility all of psychoanalysis would be irrelevant. The mistake consists in confusing the intelligibility *resulting from the overall outcome of analytic investigation* with immediate understanding *as an analytic tool*, which it is not. Indeed, understanding has its traps. One of the hazards is that, by sticking to mere intelligibility, one ends up "understanding too well," rushing to accept an appealing *coherence* of constructions, which may lead analyst and patient bitterly astray (*co-errance*).[74] This is what arises from an unconscious collusion, for example, the analytic couple agreeing that a factual event in the patient's childhood is the identifiable origin of suffering, placing far too much trust in their capacity to understand.

To understand, to be understood: the analysand naturally asks for no more and who can blame him?[75] It is the analyst's task to know how to resist this siren song and to watch out for the "prehending"

---

74 Translator's note: the French original plays on the homonymic pun between *cohérence* (coherence) and *co-errance* (going astray together), which is unfortunately lost in translation.
75 See the previously quoted text by André et al. (2012).

aspect of comprehending, which is to say for the temptation of possible control and mastery over the other, as Emmanuel Levinas has pointed out.[76] This is a problem arising when the search remains centered on only one of the two aspects of the "perceptual complex," the predicate, an orientation in which the analyst tends to identify himself with his patient, to base himself on the parallel between the familiar features of their egos with the corollary of forgetting the inassimilable residues. The question thus consists in knowing whether the analyst accepts the passibility imposed on him by the alien part of the other; whether he accepts the decentering, the putting to work of the *infantia* that extends across the analytic field and that can be viewed in terms of the model that elsewhere I have called a "Ferenczian chiasm."

Theory of Seduction and Ferenczian Chiasm

An excessive concern with coherence may have led Freud to develop the theory of seduction, fiercely defended in 1896 in his presentation to the Viennese psychiatric association, secretly abandoned in September of the following year. Let us emphasize that it was, above all, a theory of the etiology of hysteria that Freud advocated and then abandoned; the overall theory was more complex and some aspects survived the abandonment.[77] Nevertheless, it was a conception in which childhood was not yet viewed as *infantia*, which, independent of age, is a basic structure of human experience. Given the effort to understand deployed according to a positive aim, in 1896 childhood was still only a frame within which traumatic events occurred, a tender age in which there was the risk of abuse by a perverse adult. The conception of the etiology of hysteria of course found support in many cases of real abuse, but which remains on the level of the anecdotal, of individual cases.[78] Holding to this conception, is

---

76 Levinas (1992), pp. 69–70.
77 See Laplanche (1989 [1987]).
78 Op. cit.

to keep to the terrain of psychiatry, despite the reversal in which the status of hysterics shifts from being degenerates to being the victims of depraved adults. In fact, the problem remains entirely that of identifying the "prime mover" and, in addition, explaining what causes depravity in the adult...

We then enter an infinite regress (trauma resulting from depravity, itself a result of trauma, and so on indefinitely), but in my view it is one we can escape starting with Ferenczi's observations in "Confusion of the Tongues between the Adults and the Child,"[79] and slightly modifying his model to harmonize it with Laplanche model of the general theory of seduction. Then we can speak of a "Ferenczian chiasm"[80] which reveals that what traumatizes the child's soul is once again infantile sexuality, the infantile sexuality of the perverse adult. So, the child encounters the infantile: in a state of *infantia*, the child is confronted with the fact of infantile sexuality in the adult. Hence the chiasm. What happens is an intromission, a form of violence (Laplanche), or "secondary violence," to borrow Aulagnier's term. The sexual thus intromitted cannot be successfully processed psychically; it remains *actual* and becomes encysted in that same state, a traumatic core liable to repetition.

I need not go over all the arguments summoned by Freud to explain to Fliess why he has abandoned the seduction theory.[81] As we know, noticing that the unconscious memory does not "break through" in the individual anamnesis, Freud turns to phylogenesis, a most controversial hypothesis to say the least.[82] Whatever credence we lend to this hypothesis, we have to admit that Freud then searches as far as possible for a foundation in reality, trying to locate the actuality of trauma in a prehistorical temporality that nonetheless

---

79 Ferenczi (1932).
80 Scarfone (2002[2000])
81 Freud (1897), *SE* I, p. 259.
82 As evidenced by the response to Delourmel and Villa's reports at the 2013 Congress of French-Speaking Psychoanalysts, *SPP Bulletin*, n° 106 (2012).

in principle remains dateable. In that way he replicates the model of the seduction theory within a broader time scale. However, this replication is not identical: the resort to phylogenesis does away with the need for trauma in the individual history, which leads Freud to introduce infantile sexuality in *Three Essays* (1905). This in turn opens up a space where childhood can be theorized as a position of and a specific relation to the erogenous body, a relation for which the child's infantile sexual theories provide psychic coating. To some extent, this is thus a return to the paradigm developed in the *Project*.

The Sexual, the Large Infantile

In reality, since December 1896, ten months before announcing his abandonment of his "neurotica", Freud had already put the theory of seduction in peril by developing a model of successive retranscriptions of memories. From that point on, intelligibility was changed and had to take account of what Freud called "A failure of translation" [adding, "this is what is known clinically as 'repression'"] and thus of the resulting *"fueros"* constitutive of the infantile sexual domain.[83] Thus, even if the theory that follows the abandonment of 1897 ends up oriented by the concept of phylogenetically transmitted primal fantasies, as early as 1896 Freud understands, even though he does not use the term, that the position of being an *infans* provokes the theoretical efforts of the little human. The impossibility of transcribing fully what was inscribed at an earlier stage, of fully translating it into a new "language," signals the persistence of an incomprehensible trace and casts doubt on a theory premised on the memory of a "real" scene. In itself, the "transcription" model does not mark the end of Freud's belief in the memories of factual occurrences of seduction but the edifice of seduction theory in its "early form" is beginning to crack due to failures in translation that have occurred along the way. Après-coup, we can locate that unreliability on a direct line with the split

---

[83] Freud's letter to Fleiss of December 6, 1896. Freud (1985), p. 207.

between thing and predicate, between the replicable, intelligible, and therefore translatable part and the part that escapes judgment and cannot be transcribed or translated.

Let me be precise, understood in terms of our model taken from the *Project*, infantile sexuality inscribes itself outside any "developmental" frame. Without rejecting developmental psychology, or the idea that psychoanalysis may have a contribution to make in this area, I think it essential to preserve the concept of the infantile strictly in relation to its etymology. Although etymology provides no evidence, it does so happen that the *infans*, in the sense of "one who is unable to speak," regardless of age, is precisely what interests psychoanalysis. Of course, like every other psychoanalytic concept, the concept of infantile sexuality was named with the empirical child in mind, and there is no doubt that the child's concrete situation is most propitious for its emergence. But the originality of psychoanalysis consists in having a *metapsychological* perspective on the subject (as on all subjects), as opposed to a psychological one. This is to say that psychoanalytic concepts are derived from notions borrowed from empirical observation, but in a derivation that takes into account the effects of the unconscious.[84]

To ensure that these two perspectives, psychology and metapsychology, are not confused or conflated, Laplanche advocates use of the German term *Sexual* when referring to the infantile sexual which is "sexuality enlarged in the Freudian sense," as distinct from infantile sexuality understood as the *childhood* version of sexuality in general.[85] Jean Imbeault, for his part, has suggested that in Freud's writings we distinguish between the "small infantile," the evolving infantile sexuality (the child's sexuality, if you will), and the "large infantile," which cannot possibly be inscribed in a developmental sequence and

---

[84] Laplanche and Pontalis, each in his own way, accounted for this specificity of psychoanalytic thought. See Laplanche (1977 [1970]), "Derivation of the Psychoanalytic Entities," and Pontalis (1968), "Question de mots."
[85] Laplanche (2011 [2007]).

resists any form of maturation.[86] To me, these distinctions are essential to maintaining a position consistent with psychoanalytic epistemology for which observation of the developing child is not the crucial source of data—which is in no way to imply we must oppose it—but rather the crucial source is *the practice of the unconscious* in the frame of what Donnet calls "the analyzing situation."[87] This epistemological position tallies with my current focus on the "actual" dimension of the *sexual* or the *large infantile* (in this context we can overlook their differences, arguably minor) which, because they are resistant to all maturation, are located outside of temporality, or rather, are located within the atemporality Freud ascribes to the unconscious. But, because the infantile sexuality in question intervenes, acts, works, and yields effects in the human soul at all times and at any age, I think we can safely characterize it as having a specific kind of temporality, which can be named *actual time*.[88]

The Thing, a Drive-Related Residue

Given what I have said so far, I am naturally led to mention the fundamental anthropological situation as Jean Laplanche has theorized it, a situation involving seduction understood in a *generalized* (or enlarged) sense.[89] It is a situation of fundamental asymmetry in which, on account of his early psychic constitution, the child is unable to fully translate "enigmatic" messages, communications "compromised" by the adults' unconscious infantile sexuality.[90] Even though, to my knowledge, Laplanche himself never made the connection, I think that the fundamental anthropological situation aptly instantiates the Freudian model of the split between the *thing* and the

---

86 Imbeault (2000).
87 Donnet (2009 [2001]).
88 Scarfone (2002 [2000]).
89 Laplanche, "Starting from the Fundamental Anthropological Situation," in Laplanche (2011 [2007]).
90 Laplanche (1987).

predicate. Laplanche's translational model can indeed be mapped onto Freud's model of perception in the *Project*: in both cases something escapes understanding; *understanding* corresponds to Freud's *judgment* and to what Laplanche calls *translation*. The incomprehensible *thing* in the *Project* finds its counterpart in the "untranslated residues" of Laplanche's model, such residues forming the source-objects of the drive. A parallel can be drawn between the *thing* and the untranslated residues, not as a mere analogy but because both refer to a hard core which, eluding any form of understanding (of com-*prehensio*n), is nonetheless inscribed in the soul of the *infans* where it exercises its powers. This, not simply as a matter of timing (i.e. not due to the child's immaturity, the adult's perversion, etc.), but because, according to both models, the perceived carries in its very structure something ungraspable, untranslatable.

The compatibility between the two models is also supported by the fact that they both include a view of *infantia* as a position, which can never be fully overcome, of being confronted with the enigmatic aspect of the other. In this sense, the "fundamental anthropological situation" not only describes the child arriving in a world of adults, but also pertains to the *infans* inherent in everyone when confronted with the other's *infantile sexuality*. Such an *infans*, never completely gone, is and always will be confronted with the task of coping with a perceptual complex carrying a "thing-like" residue. Freud's 1895 model thus becomes clearer: whereas Freud inscribed it under the heading of cognition and reproductive thought or of remembering and judging (these are the titles of sections 16 and 17 in the *Project*), Laplanche's theory shifts the conception of the incomprehensible "thing," specifies it as a "sexual thing" without, however, ceasing to see it as a source of pressure toward translation, differentiation, and psychic elaboration or, conversely, toward enactment as discharge using the shortest possible pathway. In each case, the drive-related aspect of the "thing" is unmistakable. Here, I remain close to Freud, who wrote that drives are unknowable in themselves—in other words, that they constitute an opaque core—yet are known through their ideational representatives and affect. That is, they come with a coating of recognizable attributes. Except that such attributes, when acting as drives, are *unrecognizable*, as they have been distorted by the process of repression and by the successive returns from repression.

Asymmetrical Couples

So far we have come across the structure of the perceptual complex in two clinical entities, the actual neuroses and hysteria, and in the model of the dream. The same structure can be seen in several other contexts which are also nodal points in Freud's thought. It can be found, for example, in the way self-preservative instincts yield to sexual drives through the mechanism of leaning-on, and where the self-preservative role is taken-up by narcissism: we keep ourselves alive not only from a simple self-preservative instinct but out of self-love (and love for the object).[91] This structure is also found in the *fort/da* game in *Beyond the Pleasure Principle*. For if the child's gleeful final *da!* replaces a gloomier-sounding *fort*, we must assume the presence of an original *da* that was lost with the mother's departure and ultimately regained with her return. As long as the mother was satisfyingly present, there was no need for such a *da* to be spoken or even thought. The famous formula could thus be written: (*Da*)/*Fort*/*Da!* the parenthetical (*Da*) referring to the unsymbolized, unnamed presence.

In fact, symbolization in the *fort/da* game does not occur in the interval between the *fort* and the final *da*, it is launched instead as soon as the *fort* is uttered, insofar as this first word is what comes to replace the being-there of the mother who is now "gone."[92] The

---

91 [Tr. E.g. when a child is encouraged to eat with such words as "and now a spoonful for Mommy, now a spoonful for Daddy".]
92 Neo-Piagetian developmental psychology in fact recognizes the word/concept *gone* as a fundamental acquisition in the child's thinking, without, in truth, crediting Freud in any way. See Gopnik and Meltzoff (1997).

structure is that of a real presence which, having become unavailable, leads to a substitute representation that is at once sensory, the spool, and verbal-symbolic, the word *fort*. By designating the absence, the word already represents, symbolizes, the absent mother. In the end, the final da seems to yield only a narcissistic surplus, when the loss, acknowledged by "*ooo*" will soon be denied by the sonorous, triumphant "*aaa*."

Presenting, (Re-)Presenting, Representing

Let's stay with this famous scene a bit longer in order to show its analogy with the "double coating" at work in dreams. I said that the "thing," the unknown toward which the navel of the dream points, is first covered up by the *dream-thoughts*, which, being repressed thoughts, in their turn also behave like an opaque core which, in the context of sleep, is substituted for by the dream-images—images linked only by happenstance or compliance (*Entgegenkommen*) with the thoughts, just as somatic compliance is involved in the *soldering* encountered in the hysterical symptom. As far as the dream-work is concerned, such images are the result of a kind of 'odd job' using whatever material happens to be on hand—which brings us to the issue of presentability and representability. On the one hand, this odd-job origin of the dream-images reveal that they do not "symbolize" the dream-thoughts; on the other hand, the "double coating" of the dream's umbilical core, made up first of the dream-thoughts and then the dream-images, suggests that these images are not representations strictly speaking; rather, they are *reiterations of presentations*, which, I will refer to as *(re-)presentations*.

Dream-thoughts could be considered *representations* if only they were not obstructed by repression and prevented from being articulated because access to verbal language is deficient during sleep. Because of this aphasia, the dream-images are in play, but, as I have said, as images they do not *translate* the dream-thoughts. A true translation retains the original's semantic value despite the shift from one language to another. Had the dream-images been a translation of the dream-thoughts, there would have been no need for Freud's invention of a specific method for analyzing dreams and no need for the dreamer's associations and incidental thoughts. A resort to the kind of interpretation known as "symbolic" or "allegorical" would have sufficed, the kind of interpretation against which Freud issues "an express warning"[93] more than once, even though he concedes that, at times, we must settle for it in the absence of associations from the dreamer. Thus, in light of the fact that they arise from a use of signs and are not a return of the thing itself, it is justified to refer to dream-images as *(re-)presentations*. The parentheses and hyphen adorning the word with are not typographical coquetry; they function as a reminder that the dream-images are still tied to the *presentation*, that they "present again" and will make way for genuine *representations* only when analysis of the dream has led to the meshwork of *thoughts* from which the dream has arisen.

A similar observation can be made if we return to the *fort/da* game: the child still resorts to a sensory medium (the spool) in order to *(re-)present* the absent mother, just as he is beginning to name (i.e., *represent*) this absence. The true *representation*, however, is not acquired as long as the developing linguistic symbol remains closely tied to motility, to the act that accompanies the vocal emission, and as long as this enacted repetition—the throwing of the spool—has not given way to an act of remembering that is fully internal. The term *(re-)presentation* thus has the advantage of reminding us that, even though we are beyond the stage of raw acting out, something pertaining to *presentation* persists, something remains tied to the act, not having wholly crossed the threshold of thought. Let us note, however, that true representations are never entirely free of the effect of presence, that they will never completely stray from the sensory data. Spoken language

---

93 Freud (1900), *SE* IV, p. 459.

is itself the object of a sensory experience, and written language can rely on all sorts of figures of speech, including typographical characters, in order to convey something more and something other than the semantic content.

The persistence within representation, the persistence that I call 'motor', is not an undesirable residue. Unquestionably it reflects the embodied origins of representation, but when it is taken back up creatively, it also "actualizes" the representation (with "actual" understood here in the second sense I have proposed). It endows the representation with a driving force, supplying the kind of pleasure that accompanies thinking whenever thinking is subject to "representation" in the aesthetic sense, as in a theatrical representation. In this sense, the fort/da game is the very prototype of stagecraft, whose connection with the actuality of the unconscious thing will be explored later.

On the Extra-Analytical

For the benefit of those who feel that insisting on the difference between presentation and representation is, at best, more philosophical than psychoanalytic, let us stress the fact that Freud, with the German terms *Darstellung* and *Vorstellung*, provides an unambiguous basis for discussing the distinction.[94] But there is more. Not only is there no harm in putting a concept to work in the light of what it signifies in another semantic sphere; such comparative work is the only way to demonstrate and affirm the specific contribution of psychoanalysis. The concept of representation is a good illustration of this. I have just shown that the term *representation* is the outcome of a development which does not lead directly from a presentation endowed with a sensory charge to a representation, but passes through a stage of (re-)presenting, in the sense of *presenting anew*. This

---

[94] Laurence Kahn offers an excellent discussion of this distinction in L'*écoute de l'analyste: De l'acte à la forme* (2012), especially chapter II.

dissection is not only conceptual; it shows that if, as I claim, there is no direct movement from presentation to representation, it is because this is not a purely cognitive and solipsistic progression but involves a movement through the channels of transference, as illustrated by the case of Florence.

Put through the sieve of a psychoanalytic critique, representation is revealed always to be filled with the weight of the "thing" coming from the other, a thing of which it is the psychic representative, and which, of course, it can obscure, but a thing whose transferential reiterations reinstate the aspect of *flesh*. Psychoanalysis behaves—in this case, as always—as Freud describes it in *Introductory Lectures*:

> It is in general not such a common thing for psychoanalysis to *deny* something asserted by other people; as a rule it merely adds something new—though no doubt it occasionally happens that this thing that has hitherto been overlooked and is now brought up as a fresh addition is in fact the essence of the matter.[95]

Transference (Re-)Presents

As an intermediary stage between presentation and representation, to me *(re-)presentation* seems in harmony with the notion of "compulsion to represent" developed by Jean-Claude Rolland.[96] I will adjust this notion slightly, however, insofar as, in the context of my argument, the term "representation" can apply only to the final stage of the process theorized by Rolland, when the outcome is fully psychic and thus no longer subject to the repetition compulsion. A representation resulting merely from a compulsion would, in this sense, be a contradiction in terms. The process leading to the

---

95 Freud (1915–1917), *SE* XV, p. 45.
96 Rolland (1998), pp. 201–258.

compulsion to represent is long and complex. This is underscored by Rolland himself:

> What I refer to as the compulsion to represent is the transformation which the unconscious formation is subjected to by speech, where speech, in its development and within the limits of its language, temporarily inscribes the formation in its structure in a way that is more or less appropriate, i.e. more or less appropriating. It is indeed a representation by stages: an original representation [I would personally use the term *presentation*] that is roughly metaphorical and literally actual [...], followed by another with an improved metonymic determination and pertaining to a more indistinct temporality [Here, I would rely on the term *(re-)presentation*] [...], and then a third one that pertains, historically, to a completed temporality founded in truth [the genuine representation].[97]

In his subsequent discussion, Rolland seems to underscore what I said earlier regarding the child and the spool:

> [...] articulating word presentations with ideational contents and polymorphous affects of heterogeneous origin, spoken language places them, not yet so much in the *present* of the syntax, but in the *actuality* of the transferential experience. The latter mixes all the temporalities, blurs the ordinary boundaries of psychic functioning, and brings together the hallucinatory mode of fantasy and the articulate mode of speech.[98]

---

97 *Op. cit.*, pp. 238–239; the comments between brackets are the author's.
98 *Op. cit.*, pp. 244–245. I am adding italics to draw attention to the terms *present* and *actuality*, which make up a differential pair, an "asymmetrical couple."

With this last quotation, I am led to examine transference in the light of the distinction I propose between *(re-)presenting* and *representing*. In the transference, as we know, something of the analyst—a minor detail akin to day residues in dreams—is invested by the analysand. This provides a base, a foothold for whatever strives to be *(re-)presented* "really," circumventing the network of true symbolization. In this sense, transference is a form of repetition and acting out, but not yet a process of *representing*.

Without going into a discussion of representation (*Vorstellung*) and representative (*Repräsentanz*),[99] I would claim that adhesion to a specific meaning of the term *representation* is all the more necessary as our practice, when dealing with dreams, fantasies, and the hallucinatory sphere in general, teaches us they are not representations. We cannot refer to them saying "I represented to myself that" as they are not intellections but rather manifestations that the psyche is still relying on the sensory modalities of perception *in praesentia*. Such sensory residues do us the favor of reinstating, in the transference, a form of presence that the progress of the analysis requires, so long as we agree with Freud that no one can be destroyed *in absentia* or *in effigie*. Yet (re-)presenting is only a step toward the capacity to truly "represent" and therefore to inscribe within a symbolic network that which returns from the repressed or the excluded. Thus, as Rolland points out, transference is on the order of the actual. This underlines what I have already introduced with the example of Altichiero and examine now on the clinical level, namely that the actual has a double potentiality: just as much as it can signify an obstacle, something opaque, tending toward action as external discharge or toward somatization as internal discharge (the first stage of the actual), it is equally able to be the living source of a new impulse toward psychic elaboration, revitalizing the universe of representations because it yields an

---

[99] See all the terms affiliated to *representation* (including the entry on idea in the English translation) in Laplanche and Pontalis's *The Language of Psychoanalysis* (1973) London: Hogarth Press.

embodiment of thought, of the sort suggested by the blinding light in Altichiero's Annunciation (the second stage of the actual). This is probably what Rolland suggests when he writes, in the excerpt just quoted, that transferential actuality "brings together the hallucinatory mode of fantasy and the articulate mode of speech."

But transference plays an even more specific role in the analyzing situation. What is *(re-)presented* there is subjected to another transference, which is the transference toward articulation, toward and onto language and, more specifically onto speech, so that a pathway may open toward genuine representation. This transference toward speech results as much from the call to speak which is the fundamental rule, as from the après-coup of interpretation and its retroactive effects. Moreover, words that are uttered lead the contents of *(re-)presentation* to pass through the sensory channels,[100] so that a new cycle may be set off: each time going from auditory perception to representation—the thing/predicate split this time concerning the perceived verbal productions. With each new cycle a gain is elicited on the side of remembering.

"Lifting up" the Actual

Generalizing on the basis of what we have seen up to this point, I would say that presentation and representation are inscribed in a series of "asymmetrical couples" following the general model of the *thing* covered up by its predicate (or its attributes). In these couples, a fact initially encountered escapes the grasp of perception but is taken up and equipped with a psychic coating, which ultimately gives it a structure like this:

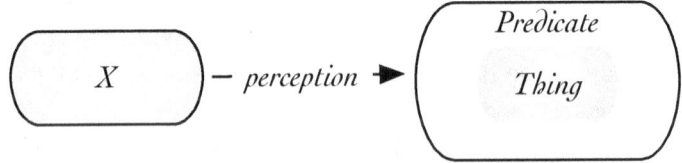

---

100 Freud (1924).

...analogous to the structure governing the relation between the actual neuroses and the psychoneuroses:

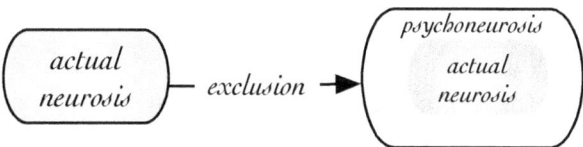

Following the same logic, in the *fort/da* game, the final *da* implies the existence of an initial un-thought element (*da*) that then is thought as *fort*, lost from sight, until reappearing in the resounding *da!* of the final stage of the game...

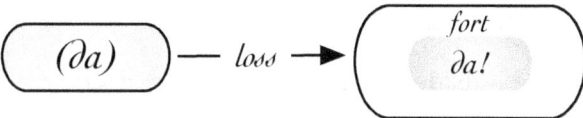

This can also be formulated as follows:

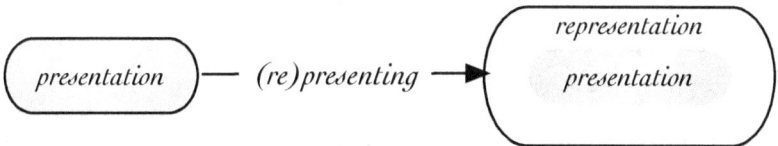

These diagrams in fact illustrate the resonance of a general process in Freud's models: the process of *Aufhebung* described by Hegel which Freud seems to have knowingly applied in at least one of his texts: "Negation." *Aufhebung* has been translated in various ways, most often as "transcending preservation", "sublation" or simply "lifting up". It can also be rendered as "suppression," provided one does not overlook the fact that what is thus suppressed is also being preserved. Hence, Freud writes:

> Negation is a way of taking cognizance of what is repressed; indeed it is already a suppression (*Auf-*

hebung) of the repression, though not, of course, an acceptance of what is repressed.[101]

This agreement with the Hegelian notion was pointed out in the 1950s by the philosopher Jean Hyppolite, at the invitation of Lacan,[102] who endorses the model when he posits that what was expelled in the inaugural affirmation returns in the real, the latter being

> ...that which subsists outside of symbolization. [...] [This real] expects nothing from speech. But it is there, identical to its existence, a noise in which one can hear anything and everything, ready to submerge with its roar what the 'reality principle' constructs there that goes by the name of the 'outside world.'

The constructed outside world is what will be called "reality." It must be distinguished from the real, on the basis that

> ... in this reality, which the subject must compose according to the well-tempered scale of his objects, the real—as that which is excised from the primordial symbolization—*is already there.*"[103]

Here is another asymmetrical couple: the real will give rise to a reality that will envelope it without in any way abolishing it. Let me note in passing that this real has a strong flavor of *actuality* ("identical to its existence") and *infantia* ("it expects nothing from speech"). Would the actual therefore be another name for the Lacanian Real? The Real is certainly actual, "always return[ing] in the same place," and it is tempting to equate the two concepts; at any rate, I find that the actual core of representation behaves like Lacan's "anchor-

---

101 Freud (1925b), SE XIX, pp. 235–236 (translation modified: Strachey translates *Aufhebung* by "lifting" in the *Standard Edition*).
102 The text of Hyppolite's commentary, with an introduction and a response by Lacan, was published in *Écrits* (1966).
103 *Op. cit.*, p. 324 [388-389] (italics in the original).

ing point" (*point de capiton*), anchoring speech in order to prevent the incessant slippage of signifiers in relation to the signified.[104] The actual core is what screws the word to the flesh and gives representation its weight of presence. Lyotard brought this out especially in terms of the distinction, within speech, between *lexis* (the articulated sentence, the enunciation, the side of verbal representation) and *phônè* (the non-articulated, self-referential dimension, like the texture of the voice) whatever in speech presents or (re-)presents itself in addition to what speech aims to *represent*.[105]

Thus "sublation" (*Aufhebung*) clearly applies to the central concepts of psychoanalysis; nevertheless, this does not make psychoanalysis "Hegelian": in all the "asymmetrical couples" that arise from the process, no synthesis is ever involved, no "ideal progress," no resolution of the asymmetry. The core "of thingness" is covered up and veiled by a variety of predicates, but it never gets to settle into any kind of final synthesis.

The Actual, A Foreign Body

If there is no "beautiful synthesis" on the psychoanalytic agenda, it might be because no psychic coating, no soldering of meaning to the *thing*, could ever defeat the alien-ness of the latter. Following Freud's method, synthesis is left to the spontaneous activity of the patient's ego and its hermeneutic function. It is not as if the analyst does not contribute, but what matters is that the analysand should ultimately become the sole signatory of his history, without counting on any "guarantee" from his analyst. As for the analysand's history, it would be misleading to think that from then on it has come to terms with the *thing*. At the end of an analysis, no one is sheltered from the effects of an encounter with or the "presence" of the other and thus of the other's inassimilable dimension. The worst outcome,

---

104 Lacan, (1954), chapter XXI.
105 Lyotard (1990).

in fact, might be to no longer ever be disturbed by the other. The disturbance caused by the other's message can never be completely avoided—fortunately, for without this disturbance, without its anarchizing effect, psychic structures would be doomed to inertia and sclerosis. One would be smothered by too much binding.[106] Lacking exposure to the disturbing thing that requires a work of psychic elaboration, the erogenous body itself would be degraded to *soma*, because if the body is connected to the drives, it is as a mediator, as a relational body. For Freud,

> the life process of the individual leads for internal reasons to an abolition of chemical tensions, that is to say to death, whereas union with a living substance of a different individual increases those tensions, introducing what may be described as fresh 'vital differences' which must then be lived off."[107]

Here, in spite of the physical–chemical terminology, we can hear an echo of *Project's* reference to some other, to some "foreign substance." It is an argument pointing toward Laplanche's notion of a source-object of the drive and in harmony with what I outlined regarding the status of the *thing* as an aspect of the drive. However, here let's not bother with the issue of the source of the drive. Whether its origin is located "inside," in the somatic processes, or "outside," in the impact of the other's message, what matters is that the drive should be viewed "as a measure of the demand made upon the soul [*das Seelenleben*] for work in consequence of its connection with the body."[108]

Let me stress that a measure of the *demand* for work is not a measure of the quantity of energy that must be *used* for this work. This does not mean that the drive itself is not endowed with pres-

---

106 Zaltzman (1997).
107 Freud, (1920), *SE* XVIII, p. 55.
108 Freud (1915a), *SE* XIV, p. 122 (translation modified).

sure (*drang*); but nothing indicates that it is this pressure that *fuels* the work demanded by the drive. Rather, what the pressure reflects is the intensity of the demand; the work demanded is on an entirely different scale. The drives present themselves as a problem the apparatus of the soul must face up to, taking the coordinates of reality into account while determining the kind of response to give. Unknowable in itself, the drives are apprehended solely by their psychic representatives: affects and representations. Inferring a drive on the basis of its psychic representatives is to recognize them as the outcome of the psychic evolution of something that, at the outset, was not psychic; but nothing compels us to locate this primary material, this something at the outset, in the somatic processes themselves. Somatic processes play their part, an essential one, as *sensible flesh*. However, just as the waters of the Ganges are not the product of the Himalayas—as rock formations—but result from the fact that snow and ice have formed at their top, the "body" that Freud inscribes in his definition of the drive can seemingly be understood not as a source, but as a mediator, an effector, a *transducer* of the transformations of what the *thing* provokes in the one who perceives it. Just as the dream-images do not translate the dream-thoughts and still less do they translate the *thing* that lies behind them, the body does not translate but *transduces* the impact of the other.[109] As it happens, the thing must be understood here as the sexual thing, as the residual of the effect of the other's enigmatic, seductive message. As Laplanche emphasizes, borrowing Hölderlin's idea, just as rivers flow in the direction of their source, the ocean, the drive "flows" toward the source-object, the other, whose impact yielded the first impulse, even if the objects the drive encounters on its path will always only be substitutes.

For Merleau-Ponty, the body "transforms ideas into things. . . . If the body can symbolize existence, it is because it actualizes it and

---

109 The notion of transduction refers to a shift or radical transformation between two heterogeneous elements or environments (e.g., the transduction of light by the retina into nerve impulses).

because it is its actuality."[110] Yet this function of actualization exposes the body to the actual, understood in its first sense as obstacle, when illness thwarts elaboration. The body itself is then actual, and its temporality is that of a "now" frozen in repetition:

> movement towards the future, towards the living present, or toward the past [...] are all somehow blocked by a bodily symptom; existence has become entangled and the body has become 'life's hiding place'. For the patient, nothing more happens, nothing takes on a sense and form in his life—or, more precisely, *nothing comes to pass but always identical "nows"*; life flows back upon itself and history is dissolved in natural time."[111]

I would say that the soul works in the opposite way: it transforms things—the bodily experience induced by the *thing*—into "ideas." This is how it responds to the demand for work, the drive. In so doing, the soul becomes differentiated, split into two domains: the *psychic* strictly speaking and the *actual*, that residue that cannot be fully transformed into a historical temporality, into the ego's autobiographical narrative. I will develop this point below.

---

110 Merleau-Ponty, (2012 [1945]), p. 167.
111 *Ibid*. Italics mine.

Actuality and Analytic Method

What seem to be highly abstract aspects of Freud's *Project* which I have discussed above in fact have significant consequences for analytic technique. Thus, Freud's view of the ego as the inhibitor of the endogenous signs of actuality has an intrinsic link with the development of the analytic method. What, we should ask, is the fundamental rule asking for when it calls for the patient to say everything that comes to mind without exercising *judgment*, and when the analyst is asked to suspend *representations of goals* in order to listen with evenly suspended attention? Nothing less than asking the ego and its inhibiting function to go on vacation – as much as possible – which means agreeing to a relative passivity in order to allow the presentation of mental contents that carry signs of actuality although they come from within. Psychic reality, thus marked by its "actuality," then appears in all its fecundity, its effectivity (*Wirklichkeit*), far beyond a merely subjective perspective. In fact, it might be appropriate to speak of "psychic actuality" to highlight that it has little to do with the reality confirmed by reality testing. At the very end of *The Interpretation of Dreams*, Freud notes that psychic reality "is a particular form of existence not be confused with *material* reality."[112] In fact, psychic reality cannot be subjected to reality testing; to the contrary, it best manifests itself when the function of judgment is suspended.

---

112 Freud (1900), *SE* IV, p. 620. [Tr. In addition Freud distinguishes 'psychic reality' from subjective reality in general, that is from "transitional or intermediate thoughts."]

The fundamental rule implicitly asks the two partners to give license to "dream thinking" ("*pensée rêvante*" Pontalis), to fantasy, which pertains to the hallucinatory sphere. They are asked to suspend reality testing but also—only up to a certain point, as it is not completely achievable—to suspend the inhibiting function of the ego in charge of what Marie Leclaire and I have called "actuality testing."[113] Thus, it is not only representations of goals, or judgment, that is suspended; rather, analyst and analysand are invited to tolerate a state of being suspended between what is no longer the reality yielded by the exercise of judgment, and yet not fully in the hallucinatory mode which would entail a radical dismissal of the ego. In this way, they find themselves in a state of psychic weightlessness from which they can emerge once belief in external reality has reclaimed its rights and they shift from primary belief, whose actuality conforms to the hallucinatory mode, to secondary belief (belief in reality) arising from judgment. Being suspended between these two kinds of belief offers the best chance of reconfiguring the psychic, of bringing about change in the analytic sense. What takes place is a shift from the actual in a raw state to that other state of the actual that I described at the very beginning: the impediment of blinding light is replaced by a light that endows the experience with depth and pathways to sublimatory liberation.

Aiming for such suspensions is what makes the establishment of the analytic situation a reestablishment: analyst and analysand are urged to allow for the play of the *infans*, to reconnect with *passibility*, a deliberate, desired, chosen passivity that is sustained by going against the current of spontaneous tendencies. For the duration of the session, the analyst and his patient are encouraged to adopt a disposition likely to make them recapture that state of *infantia* in which clearly differentiating between outside and inside, between fiction and reality, is not required. In this Winnicottian space, as may have

---

113 Leclaire and Scarfone (2000). See "Actuality and Reality" page 104 above.

been guessed, I deliberately use the verb "play" because it is a disposition quite similar to the *playing* of childhood or of theatrical play.[114] Such playing, such softening of the borders between actuality and reality, is present as an analysis begins. This is sense in which I agree with Donnet's notions of "analytic site" and "analyzing situation": they reveal that, before making any formulation of any kind, the analyst is expected to set up the conditions in which the analysis may operate as if by itself, in "auto-" mode:

> The analyzing situation . . . takes the form of a structure integrating the analysand-analyst couple in its capacity for self-organization, as well as the dynamic processes of its disorganizations-reorganizations.[115]

Crisis of Representation

In the face of these suspensions, the ego is quick to put up resistance to counter the disorganizations-reorganizations they entail; it does not easily let itself be put on hold, and is reluctant to abandon the compromises, however unstable they may be, which it has arrived at over the course of a lifetime. In some cases, as Winnicott points out, the subject altogether lacks the capacity to play. There is no need to cite extreme cases to illustrate this as even for patients who have the greatest natural ability to play the effects of analytic decomposition can induce a "crisis of representation." Poised on the cusp between analytic process and resistance to decomposition, the analyzing situation gives rise to the appearance, more or less pronounced, of repetition. Freud says the patient repeats instead of remembering.[116] Let us refer the verb "remembering" back to the way Freud uses it in the *Project* in which he says the work of remembering is involved

---

114 Leclaire and Scarfone (2004)
115 Donnet (2009), p. 36.
116 Freud (1914a).

The Unpast

in understanding of attributes, of the predicate, and that because the predicate "can be traced back to information from [the subject's] own body."[117] This suggests, *a contrario*, that the analysand who repeats instead of remembering is precisely forgetful of himself, of his own body and of his history *as history*.

This crisis of representation sets in motion not only an impersonal force tending toward action-discharge, but also a temporality that is itself tied to this form of action, *actual time*. Because the work of decomposition the analytic process instigates is a work of de-translation, a sort of peeling off of the ego's past acquirements, all the preceding translations, theories, and representations are subjected to what de M'Uzan describes in terms of disturbance, of economic scandal,[118] a prerequisite for change in the analysis. Such a disturbance can be considered from the angle of temporal unrest. The Gestalt, the adequate form of speech and its chronological temporality, is disturbed by the irruption of an "other time," an actual time, the time of repetition, the time of action: a time outside of chronology. To return to Merleau-Ponty: "nothing comes to pass but always identical 'nows.'" Whatever appeared to belong to the past from a chronological perspective, now turns out never really to have gone away. I suggest that this temporality be referred to as the *unpast* (*l'impassé*), retaining its status as an *impasse* in the subject's life.

If once again we refer to Altichiero's fresco and its *oculus*, we see that just as the oculus, piercing the surface of the Oratory's façade, first appeared as an actual problem likely to be detrimental, similarly, the emergence of an acted-out repetition, which appears "with such unwished-for exactitude,"[119] can, if worst comes to worst, derail the analytic project. But just as the painter's integration of the opening into the fresco endowed the painting with special intensity

---

117 Freud (1950 [1895]), SE I, p. 331 (translation modified).
118 de M'Uzan (1994), pp. 115–128.
119 Freud (1920), SE XVIII, p. 18.

and depth—a luminous *actuality* in the service of aesthetic or spiritual experience—in the same way, the irruption of the actual in the course of the analysis, interrupting representation, is a disturbance required for the possibility of change because it confers on the analytic experience, through the transference, all of its "gravity."

As may be clear, I am merely agreeing with what Freud says in his two texts on transference (1912 and 1914) when he writes that "it is impossible to destroy anyone *in absentia* or *in effigie*" and that the irruption of the transference in the treatment is like a fire that breaks out in a theater and marks the end of the representation...[120]

Transference, Atemporality and Actual Time

In the two texts just mentioned, transference phenomena are treated from two perspectives at two different times. The first, in "The Dynamics of Transference" of 1912, seems concerned above all with elucidating a hidden meaning, based on the premise of intelligibility, whereas the second, in "Observations on Transference-Love" of 1914, pays more attention to enactment. In the 1912 essay, transference phenomena are conceived of as *reprints* of "stereotype plates" and consequently can be seen as on the side of the representable and thus of the psychic. Only the very last paragraph refers to the actual dimension in the form of what I call (re-)presentations. Though the passage has often been quoted, I must present it once again:

> The unconscious impulses do not want to be remembered in the way the treatment desires them to be, but endeavour to reproduce themselves in accordance with the atemporality of the unconscious and its capacity for hallucination. . . . It cannot be disputed that controlling the phenomena of transference presents the psycho-analyst with the greatest difficulties.

---

[120] Freud (1912), SE XII, p. 108 and (1914b), SE XII, p. 162.

> But it should not be forgotten that it is precisely they that do us the inestimable service of making the patient's hidden and forgotten erotic impulses actual and manifest. For when all is said and done, it is impossible to destroy anyone *in absentia* or *in effigie*.[121]

I am tempted, as one might guess, to underline the adjective "actual" (*aktuelle*) that Freud applies to the love impulses revived by the transference. Even though, on a first reading, "making actual" seems to be used in the banal sense of "returning to the present of the analysis," the first half of the quotation suggests that the reproduction of this "present" has something to do with the atemporality of the unconscious... This combination of "present" with atemporality must be emphasized. It seems me to justify another way of defining the Actual, this time as an "atemporal present." Though the present is inscribed in the sequence past-present-future, and therefore inscribed in time in the most everyday sense of the term,[122] let us recall, at the risk of revisiting well-known facts, the difficulty inherent in the notions of 'past', 'present', and 'future'. Already in the year 400, Augustine wrote:

> How can the past and future be, when the past no longer is, and the future is not yet? As for the present, if it were always present and never moved on to become the past, it would not be time, but eternity.[123]

The last sentence of this passage seems to converge with the notion I am trying to affirm here: the notion of actual time. Analyzing

---

121 Freud (1912), *SE* XII, p. 108.
122 Let us stress that the time I am referring to here is only time as it presents itself in the lived experience and in the psychic apparatus (or the apparatus of the soul), and not the cosmological time of physics which, as we know, has been the object of a conceptual revolution when, from the "measure of movement" it once constituted in the Aristotelian tradition, it became integrated, with Einstein's relativity, into a space-time continuum.
123 Augustine (1961), p. 264.

the three times of chronology, Augustine observes that the present cannot be endowed with duration and thus cannot be divisible, as it would instantly break up into past and future. The present, he points out, is therefore always moving on to become the past, or else it would be eternity. Now we have just seen that the work of analysis leads to the emergence of repetition. What returns is only seemingly "in the present," since if it were the present, it would soon "become the past" and therefore cease returning. Yet it returns, it repeats itself, precisely because it has failed to become part of the past. Unable to become past, it cannot be present either; or it must be thought of as a very specific kind of present, not eternal but "atemporal," as we inferred from the statements of Freud that I have quoted, an "atemporal present" that corresponds with what I call "actual time" or, better even, *impassé* or the unpast. This leads to revisiting and correcting our view of the atemporality of the unconscious: it is not a total absence of time but a time that is "other," a time "that does not pass" to borrow Pontalis's phrase. This also seems to tally with Green's statement that "the atemporality of the unconscious thus signifies, in fact, the atemporality of Eros, the persistence of traces laid down in earliest infancy at the heart of the psyche which still bears its *ever active* marks."[124]

How does this unpast (*impassé*) relate to the adjective *zeitlos* (timeless, atemporal) that Freud uses and specifies? Let us look at his well-known description from 1915:

> The processes of the system *Ucs.* are *atemporal*; i.e. they are not ordered temporally, are not altered by the passage of time; they have no reference to time at all. Reference to time is bound up ... with the work of the system Cs.[125]

The fact that processes in the unconscious should not be *ordered* temporally is not hard to envisage; it is perfectly in keeping with the

---

124 Green (2002 [2000]), p. 151 (italics mine; translation modified).
125 Freud (1915c), SE XIV, p. 187.

logic of primary processes. We can even make an addition to Freud's phrase: they are ordered neither temporally nor in any other way. What is left is to understand what Freud means when he asserts that the processes in question "are not altered by the passage of time; they have no reference to time at all."

The first thing to mention is that to speak of alterations arising from the "passage of time" is at the same time to say too much—the idea of a passage of time is arguable in itself—and not enough, as it remains an abstract regarding "how" such alterations come about. What, in practice, is alteration by time, alteration that unconscious contents are not subjected to? How does "time" operate to alter conscious processes, to subject them to its wear and tear?

In truth, the idea that unconscious contents are immune to the wear and tear of time is not a new one. It has in fact been addressed rather specifically in *Studies on Hysteria* in which Freud, far from speaking of atemporality, he posits that the hysteric's psyche comprises archives "in correct and proper order" following a variety of modalities, including linear chronological order.[126] The absence of wear, the freshness of the elements brought to light by the therapeutic work, is noted in the famous statement from the *Preliminary Communication* which opens the book: "*Hysterics suffer mainly from reminiscences*".[127] The wearing down of such reminiscences brought back to consciousness is understood as stemming from affective discharge (abreaction), but

> even if it has not been abreacted, [the memory] enters the great complex of associations, it comes alongside other experiences, which may contradict it, and is subjected to rectification by other representations.[128]

This provides a more detailed account of what elsewhere Freud refers to simply as the "passage of time." What presents itself in

---

126 Freud (1895b), *SE* II, pp. 287–288.
127 Breuer and Freud (1893), *SE* II, p. 7.
128 *Loc. Cit.*, p. 9 (translation slightly modified).

1915 as the unexplained outcome of the absence of time in the unconscious thus seems to be thought of as the result of being subjected to primary process. What keeps the repressed from being "altered by the passage of time," is in fact the flexibility of the links and the absence of logical contradiction in the primary process that protects the repressed from the wear and tear of time. Its contents persist, as fresh as on the first day, by virtue of being excluded from any form of exchange with representations likely to alter them. They are sheltered, not from time considered abstractly, but from the principle of contradiction that regulates secondary processes. So we need not deny them all temporal dimension; we see them as immersed in an "other time."

Here one could object: if primary processes alone account for the absence of alteration by the passage of time, why the insistence on the term "time"? There are several reasons. *The first* is that if psychic processes are not locatable in space, except metaphorically, in any rigorous discussion of them we are left with the only other category: time. Freud himself, in the last period of his work, deplored the fact that he had

> made too little theoretical use of [the] fact, established beyond any doubt, of the unalterability by time of the repressed. This seems to offer an approach to the most profound discoveries.[129]

The second reason is that the unconscious involves work, displacement, transference, repetition, and expending energy, each of which entails a temporal dimension. *Third*, there is a spontaneous tendency to locate in the past the origin of the material that, thanks to the work of analysis, emerges on the surface of the psychic. As we have seen, our metapsychological reflections contradict that naive intuition. In 1933, revisiting the thesis of the atemporality of wishful impulses (of the id, in this instance), Freud writes that those impulses

---

129 Freud (1932), SE XXII, Lecture XXXI, p. 74. (translation modified)

can only be recognized as belonging to the past, can only lose their importance and be deprived of their investment of energy, when they have been made conscious by the work of analysis, and it is on this that the therapeutic effect of analytic treatment rests to no small extent.[130]

This is another reason to propose the term "unpast" (*impassé*), which accommodates the fact that it is not a true past, that it continues to act in the present; yet it is also is *capable* of becoming part of the past. We can also see that for Freud the work of analysis certainly has the effect of constituting a true past, an idea embraced by other authors important to me.[131] Yet, unless we make time starting from nothing, it is necessary to posit a primary material that would somehow be "proto-temporal," so to speak. *Fourth*, it is clear that when Freud describes the unconscious as *zeitlos* (atemporal), he is thinking of the time of clocks, the time of chronology, the time of duration oriented by the irreversible arrow of time ("time that flows"). Yet a whole other part of Freud's theory concedes, if not some reversibility of the arrow of time, at least a form of temporality which is more complex and includes loops of action après-coup (I will return to this point): this is not the quantified, unidirectional time of the clock, but is nonetheless a category of time.

An Actual Clock...

Freud's distinction between the *Cs* and *Ucs* systems does not entail a radical split but, rather, recognizes that there is circulation between the two in the form of sublation (*Aufhebung*)[132] as in the case of negation. Without such sublation, nothing could ever be said about the *Ucs*. The question that arises is: how can an atemporal element

---

130 *Ibid.*
131 de M'Uzan (1974); P. Aulagnier (1989).
132 See footnote #101 on page 124

present itself, with the element's negation, in the *Pcs-Cs* subsystems, where time is taken into account, without a reversal of its repression? The question seems to find a natural answer in the phenomenon of repetition—or, more precisely, of (re-)presentations. Isn't the *loop* formed by what (re-)presents itself a cyclical form of time different from the time that is said to "flow"?

If we look closely we see that the two forms of time, the linear and the circular, are inseparable. In the *Pcs-Cs*, we are in a world where time counts and is counted. Yet how does one measure a linear, chronometric time whose line points in the direction of the infinity of what is yet to come (*à-venir*)? With a clock or an hourglass but, in any case, with something that functions on the basis of... repetition in a loop! Indeed, we cannot *keep a count* of chronological time, which appears to be running in a straight line, without juxtaposing it with a motion *that repeats itself*. Consequently, the very instruments used to measure time would lose their function if time affected them. In this sense, they are atemporal.

Naturally, any particular clock is itself "dated" and in this sense, like any other object, is inscribed in time; but when *this* clock rusts away, its function will be taken up by another of its empirical incarnations, by a new clock. Individual clocks may pass away, but the function, the "clock" process itself, is not affected by time. Étienne Klein writes that in fact "any clock disguises time with a mixture of motion and duration which induces us to conflate it with time."[133]

Thus a clock is a technical subterfuge which, in so far as it is a function or a process, is itself removed from time; but we believe we can "see" the passage of time in the motion of the clock's hands, as

---

133 Klein *Chronos: How Time Shapes Our Universe* (2005 [2004]), p. 22. The question of time as such is most difficult to grasp and that is not what I am trying to do here. I only want to shift the question of the atemporality of the *Ucs*. a little bit, by suggesting that what Freud seems to have in mind when he puts this idea goes further than, is other than, the *duration* of time as understood by modern physics. As far as I can tell, in the context of the latter, it would be impossible to posit anything outside the space-time continuum.

if we were on the shoulder of road it travels, watching it go by. As if we were itting on the banks on the River Time, so to speak, where we have placed a waterwheel whose consecutive turns mark off quantifiable units in the continuity of its course: seconds, minutes, hours, etc. This metaphor is not as far from Freud's thought as it may seem. Remember that in more than one place Freud himself proposes as a mechanism to represent time, a device that *periodically*, repeatedly, deploys its antennae, palpates, and tastes samples from the outer world.[134] So there is no radical separation between temporality and atemporality in the apparatus of the soul. The model of the clock suggests that at the same time there is an inseparability of the *Pcs-Cs* chronology (of measured time) and the atemporality of the *Ucs* (the repetition that measures time), *and also* an operational distinctness between the two systems.[135]

Whatever we do, we can only think in terms of time, and whenever we try to picture its absence, we are bound to resort to metaphors, analogies, or impossible figures, such as some of Escher's prints or Saul Steinberg's cartoons, like the one featuring an alarm clock on the face of which the usual numbers are all replaced by the word NOW.

---

134 Freud (1920, 1925a, 1925b).
135 My position seems aligned with that of François Gantheret (1990, p. 150), who suggests that the *Ucs* works within space and its product is atemporal, whereas the *Pcs.-Cs.* works within time and its product is spatial.

Thus, the hands on this clock can turn all they want but time will not seem to pass. Indeed, at all times the face displays that it is now… "now." Despite its absurd humor, such an image in fact aptly illustrates an "atemporal present," an actual time in the most elementary form. Only by affixing numbers to it—differential marks, conventional *signs, representations*, i.e. a psychic coating—can we generate the impression and the measure of a time which passes.

Of course, to mark time, the clock must be endowed with motion. Étienne Klein writes that the clock "dresses up" time with motion and thus spatializes it.[136] In this way we have another instance of "double coating" like the one we encountered with dreams. The signs (even arbitrary ones) that indicate the hours "dress up" the movements of the clock; but the motion itself is a "dressing up" of time. Could this parallel be extended to the point of suggesting that the unconscious *thing* is atemporal only for the simple and unsettling reason that it is time itself? The limits of this work mean I must leave this question unanswered.

Returning to the metaphor of the clock, we are in the presence of three basic elements—immutability, motion, and signs (representations)—ordered along two distinct dimensions of the apparatus of the soul: a dimension of the "atemporal present," characterized by repetition, tending toward a reinstatement of the same due precisely to its indifference (in the ideal) to measured time; let us refer to this dimension as *actual*. This first dimension is inseparable from the second, in which, by virtue of the *(re-)presentation* and then *representation* of the motion, the marking of a difference will occur, thus yielding the impression of a "passage of time," a chronology. On the basis of this represented time, more complex motions can be envisioned, including the retroactive motions of après-coup: let us refer to this second dimension as the *psychic* dimension.

---

[136] Klein (2005 [2004]), p. 20.

Psychic, Soulical

The difference between the psychic and the soulical (*animique*) sphere has only recently been introduced into psychoanalytic discourse.[137] It arises from the recent French translations of Freud's complete works. The French translators could not determine with certainty whether Freud actually made a clear conceptual distinction between the two terms; however, they believed that a tendency could be perceived in Freud's differential use of the words *Seele* and *Psyche* and of the corresponding adjectives, *seelisch* and *psychisch*. "Psyche" and "psychic" have consistently been used as a pair to translate both terms, but the French translators have opted to use "soul"/"soulical" (*âme/animique*) and "psyche"/"psychic" (*psyché/psychique*). They arguably noticed that the adjective "psychic" (*psychisch*) appears mostly when Freud discusses something relatively structured, so that *psychisch* "qualifies more readily terms like *Instanz, Organisation, Topik, Material, Repräsentant* or *Vertretung*, and the terms *Energie, Realität* or *Trauma* quasi exclusively," whereas "*seelisch* most often qualifies *Akt, Leben, Phänomen, Regung, Tätigkeit, Vorgang* or *Zustand*."[138]

For the time being, this is just a possible avenue to explore, and its validity would need to be checked through a closer examination of the specific contexts in which the terms appear. Yet the difference between soulical and psychic could be, however provisionally, of interest to us. If the term psychic does indeed turn out

---

137 Translator's note: I have opted for the adjective "soulical" to translate *animique*, its French equivalent. The adjective "soulish" is another option, but "soulical" establishes a clearer parallel between "psyche/psychic" and "soul/soulical," announcing their status as an "asymmetrical couple," which the author further develops. In the *Standard Edition*, Strachey tends to translate *seelisch* by "of the mind" or "mental," thus removing any reference to the soul. As for the recent psychoanalytic debate over the translation of *seelisch* and *psychisch*, it has to my knowledge not been addressed in the anglophone literature until now.

138 Bourguignon et al. (1989), p. 78. [The German terms associated with *psychisch* are, in the order in which they are listed: agency, organization, topography, material, representative, representative, energy, reality, and trauma; the terms associated with *seelisch* are act, life, phenomenon, excitation, functioning, process, condition.]

to correspond to the organization in agencies, to the topographic and structural models, to the play of 'ideational representatives' and representations, and thus corresponds to the delay introduced by the work of elaboration, then the psychic can be seen in terms of a complex temporal course, including the temporality of *après-coup*, capable of reorganization and retroactivity, as revealed unequivocally the clinical work with the psychoneuroses. The "soulical"—which is to say the sphere, in which we find action (*Akt*), life (*Leben*), activity or functioning (*Tätigkeit*), the process (*Vorgang*) or the state, the condition (*Zustand*)—would, in contrast, be endowed with a different, more basic temporality which would act as the generative stratum of the psychic. Differentiation would take place within it, proceeding along the lines I have specified as the work of (re-)presentation, work which conjures up the circular mechanics of the clock metaphor. What thus emerges, totally congruent with what we have seen up to now, is another asymmetrical couple in which the psychic is not opposed to the soulical but generated by it. The psychic constantly springs up from the soulical as long as nothing blocks the process of differentiation, that is, as long as what is (re-)presented finds a response that allows the work of remembering (in the sense I have specified). I venture to suggest that the reinsertion of the actual, that is, the shift from moment 1 to moment 2 that I have described, marks the difference between the soulical and the psychic, as illustrated below:

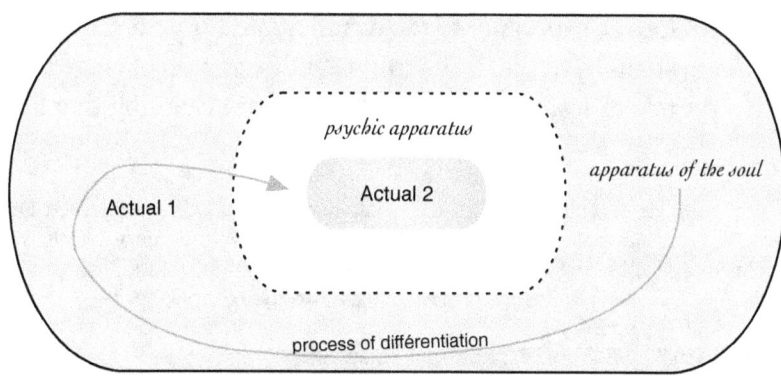

Ultimately, the soulical and the psychic are only more or less distinct in terms of being more or less differentiated (hence the porous borders between them). The psychic differentiates itself according to the role the actual plays within it by virtue of being functionally integrated. The actual can be found in the psychic apparatus in the sense of *Aufhebung*, at once transcended and preserved, like the oculus at the heart of the Annunciation. The delineation between soulical and psychic is based neither on location nor on contents; but rather, a temporal distinction in the sense of the distinction between the two moments of the actual. Here again moment 1 is sublated, transcended/preserved, in moment 2, the actual temporality being thrust into, reinstated within, psychic time as an anchoring element, as a point of captation (*point de capiton*).[139] Such anchoring endows the psychic with its consistency, with the weight of its presence, without which it could drift along indefinitely.

*

Laurence Kahn, who has serious reservations regarding the neologism "soulical" (*animique*), as well as about the psychic/soulical partition suggested by the French translators of the *Œuvres complètes*, has nonetheless shown that in chapter VII of *The Interpretation of Dreams* Freud distinguishes between *Seele* and *Psyche*.[140] She points out that at this stage of Freud's thinking, he attributes the adjective *seelisch* ("soulical") to the *instrument*, but *psychisch* (psychic) to the *productions* of the soul (*Seele*), especially to the differentiated psychic agencies or systems: systems in which, let us stress, "the excitation passes through ... in a particular *temporal* sequence."[141] Without claiming that Freud

---

139 [Tr. '*point de capiton*' relates to the neologism '*capitation*' about which Dylan Evans write"... adopted by Lacan in 1948 to refer to the imaginary effects of the specular image...[having] the double sense... of 'captivation' ...[and] 'capture'" *An Introductory Dictionary of Lacanian Psychoanalysis*, Routledge, 1996, p. 20.]
140 Kahn (1993), pp. 33–54.
141 Freud (1900), *SE* IV, p. 537; Kahn, *op. cit.*, p. 47.

has always upheld this view,[142] it suits me in this context, as it seems to me to confirm the point I made earlier, namely, that a sequential temporal course does exist in the *psychic* unconscious. If I return to the metaphor of the clock, this is what occurs when *differential marks* are displayed on the face of the clock: they then *produce* the impression of the passage of time, whereas for the *machine* as an object, each unit of motion is identical to itself. In fact, in terms of the soulical sphere that is coming into view, there is not even a unity of time or motion, the machine, the clock, being immersed in an "actual" temporality, in a time that does not pass. Only psychic elaboration, thanks to the complexity it introduces, can transform this actual temporality into a time where chronology and après-coup become thinkable.[143]

Jean-Claude Rolland seems to be in full agreement with this when he underlines the fact that the apparatus of the soul is more extended than the psychic apparatus,[144] the latter being characterized, among other things, by the predominance of language, an organized and organizing element, a factor of differentiation if ever there was one. By holding that the psyche is embedded in the body, Françoise Coblence situates language as a bridge between body and psyche,[145] which concurs with the idea of differential markers affixed to the face of the clock, without which it would always dispaly 'now'. In reality, Coblence's idea is more complex, for while language might be a bridge between body and psyche, still, in her view, "for Freud the life of the soul, the life of lived experiences, is the equivalent of the psyche."[146] This calls for a few qualifications because, as Kahn has pointed out, a confusion has occurred in the terms inherited from Greek and Latin. The French word *âme* ("soul") comes from the Latin *anima*, a transla-

---

142 In a personal exchange, Kahn has assured me that such is not the case.
143 Chronology and après-coup are naturally two different things, but it is thanks to the former that the latter can be envisioned.
144 Rolland (2000), p. 22.
145 Coblence (2010), p. 1335.
146 *Op. cit.*, p. 1288.

tion of the Greek word *psuchè*; however, *âme* ended up connoting the notion of "animation," which could not have been inferred from the Greek word.¹⁴⁷ After a thorough study of Freud's use of the term *Seele*, Kahn makes an illuminating statement:

> In short, when the theory of the drive requires the border between the somatic and the psychic in order to maintain the gap between excitation and representation, the soul, in contrast, *strides across* with elation, jettisoning, among other things, the old opposition between body and soul, so as to ensure, empirically, the *unity* of animation.¹⁴⁸

Regardless of whether *seelisch* is translated more or less adequately in the *Œuvres complètes*, Kahn seems to subscribe to the idea that *Seele*, the soul, is on the side of the continuum, of the less differentiated, in which there is no distinction from the body. This, in my view, might justify Coblence's translation of Freud's famous aphorism "Psyche is extended" as "Psyche is bodily." Indeed, psyche is extended inasmuch as it rests on the body-soul unity or continuum. That continuum is indivisible in Freud's conceptualization, but it becomes differentiated into psychic agencies or systems, characterized by distinct temporalities, with language operating as a bridge. By endorsing the phrase "the life of the soul," Coblence also stresses that the psyche is the result of a differentiation, a specialization within the more "foundational" whole constituted by the soulical sphere. But she suggests even more: the psyche refers to that *particular time* when the soul is truly endowed with *animation*. Coblence seems to say that obstructing the *life* of the soul implies an obliteration of the psychic, degrading the body to mere *soma*, its temporality becoming repetitive, actual—death seizing the living.

---

147 Kahn (1993), *op. cit.*, p. 33 et seq.
148 *Op. cit.*, pp. 40–41 (italics mine).

The concepts of soulical and psychic, allow me to build on the distinction I drew at the beginning of this text between two moments of the actual. The actual in its raw state, the object of the work of differentiation and integration, would belong to the undifferentiated soulical domain; the other moment of the actual, the moment when it is found embedded at the heart of a more successful elaboration of which it is, as it were, the pulsating source, that moment belongs to the psychic domain. It belongs to the psychic domain, in the manner of an inclusion which is at once "transcended and preserved" as in my diagrams. But let me stress that the actual as the core of the psychic is an inclusion that is in no way inert. Quite the opposite: the time of action, the actual, is what acts and what can subvert the beautiful constructions of the psyche, always too symmetrical and too harmonious to be true. This is precisely what will be unveiled in the transference.

Clinically speaking, the distribution between the soulical and the psychic seems to me to be what permits the formulation of a therapeutic project, even when the process of psychic differentiation has been elaborated either insufficiently or not at all, as in psychosomatic disorders. The soulical that forms the backdrop is open to being animated and consequently, through therapeutic techniques I cannot discuss here, to be differentiated to various degrees. In the most common analytic practice, the distinction between the two temporalities corresponds to the two levels of transference as described by Freud in 1912 and 1914. Insofar as it provides new editions, new printings (as they say in the printing business), of stock "boilerplate," the transference is in the psychic domain. On the other hand, the more fundamental form of transference arising from the soulical sphere would be what sets the house on fire: a transference in action, entirely *in praesentia*, a transference for which representation is lacking. Laplanche has suggested a distinction between "filled-in" transference (which I would locate on the psychic side, "actual 2") and "hollowed-out" transference[149] (which I would locate on the soulical side, "actual I"). In the hollowed-out transference, the enigma dwelling at the heart of the other's message is (re-)presented, the hollow of representation wreaking havoc with the associative flow and leading to the actual experience of otherness.[150] Such distinctions are not merely theoretical; they require a different "handling" (as Freud puts it) by the analyst.

---

149 Laplanche (1999 [1991])
150 Scarfone (2011b)

The Actual, *Après-coup*, and the Past

My view of the transference in terms of actuality seems quite in accord with Freud's statements on the subject in his 1912 and 1914 texts. There, the transference is compared to a fire that brings the theatrical representation to an end,[151] but one could equally say that it puts an end to representation itself. "No more playing!" seems to be the rule when such a transference arises. The actual then appears in all the polysemy possessed by the term "actuality": it includes actions but also evokes a topical form of temporality, especially in French, in which the term can even refer to "current events." However, in the latter sense, "actuality" generally denotes what is taking place topically and, as it is liable to change at the whim of the headlines, it is quick to become obsolete. Conversely, as we saw earlier, actuality can be understood as something much different from the present of chronology, namely, an atemporal present. As in Steinberg's clock, the temporality of the actual is a "permanent now." Freud gives some evidence of this in another major text, from 1914, "Remembering, Repeating and Working-Through," when, in two contiguous sentences, he formulates two *contrasting* stances with regard to his characterization of the work in the analytic session:

> in drawing attention to the compulsion to repeat
> ... we have only made it clear to ourselves that the
> patient's state of being ill cannot cease with the begin-

---
151 Freud (1915 [1914b]), *SE* XII, p. 162.

> ning of his analysis, and that *we must treat his illness, not as an event of the past, but as a present-day force* [*eine Aktuelle Macht*]. This state of illness is brought, piece by piece, within the field and range of operation of the treatment, and while the patient experiences it *as something real and contemporary* [*Aktuelles*], we have to do our therapeutic work on it, which consists in a large measure in *tracing it back to the past*.[152]

A two-step process: we do not address the illness as something historical; it cannot be *recognized* as "an event of the past" (Freud will re-state this in 1932) but rather as "a present-day force"; yet, paradoxically, *our task* consists in tracing things back to the past. For Michel de M'Uzan the point of the analysis is indeed to *constitute* the category of the past.[153] Winnicott concurs when, in "Fear of Breakdown", he asserts that the work of the analysis is to put the experience of breakdown "into the past tense," after bringing it into the zone of experience "in the present."[154] This will be the work of the transference, which does not consist in sterile repetition, in that it is also a form of transport, of displacement. Something repeats itself in it, making the analytic situation the site not of a narration but of an acting-in that is also the advent of a presence, a (re-)presentation, not a representation.

(Re-)presentation can serve two functions. The first is a transferential function in the sense of the "stereotype plates" of the 1912 text. In this case, transferential repetition will yield an elaboration that the analyst's interventions can facilitate when he reactivates the (re-)presentations, guiding the analysand toward representation and symbolization without encountering too many pitfalls. This would coincide with the level we have designated as "psychic," and with

---

152 Freud (1914a), p. 191 (italics mine).
153 de M'Uzan (1974), *op. cit.*
154 Winnicott (1964), p. 91.

The Actual, Après-coup, and the Past

Laplanche's "filled-in transference."[155] The other function is one of discharge. This would consist in acted-out repetition, an *Agieren* in the radical sense. According to Pontalis, if the analyst is not careful, this kind of repetition presents the risk of generating "an interpretive stuffing that merely responds to what feels like a vacuity, a hollowing-out."[156] The analyst would then expend himself in vain in his attempt to solder meaning to what is nothing but quantity.

In the same vein, in agreement with de M'Uzan, we must distinguish between the "repetition of the same" and the "repetition of the identical."[157] While repetition of the identical can only be conceived of asymptotically,[158] by contrast it highlights the characteristics of repetition of the same. However minimal, the displacements that occur in repetition of the same introduce a "butterfly effect" into the progression of the analysis, as it is often referred to in relation with the "theory of nonlinear dynamic systems" sometimes called "chaos theory."[159] "The flap of a butterfly's wing in the South Pacific can set off a tornado in Texas" is said by way of emphasizing that complex systems (i.e., systems endowed with nonlinear dynamics) are highly sensitive to even minute variations of the initial conditions. This principle may equally well be applied to the complex systems in which psychic processes operate, as Freud keenly remarked about repression.[160]

Such sensitivity to "minute modifications" underscores the distinction suggested by de M'Uzan, in so far as a small difference in repetition opens up substantial possibilities even though they may

---

155 Laplanche (1991).
156 Pontalis (1974), p. 13.
157 de M'Uzan (1970).
158 Scarfone (2007).
159 Pragier and Faure-Pragier (2007).
160 "[A] little more or a little less distortion alters the whole outcome [of repression]", Freud writes (1915b, *SE* XIV, p. 150). Freud thus seems familiar with "chaos theory" as it is now called but which was formulated by Poincaré more than a century ago. See Biche (1998), p. 131. http://mapageweb.umontreal.ca/scarfond/T9/9-Biche.pdf

only be confirmed later in the course of the analysis. In my view, the distinction between the same and the identical resonates with the double potentiality of the actual: as the sign of a degeneration in the direction of the soulical from a deficiency of the psychic processes (actual neuroses, "slaves of quantity"[161]), or, conversely, as the source of a new impulse toward elaboration, or even creativity, the repetition of the same leading to psychic elaboration. In short, the actual repeats itself but not always identically: the status of the act that embodies it will depend on that difference, however infinitesimal, which will bring about significant consequences in psychic evolution.

Actuality of Pain and Après-coup

The transference brings back the actual and, as repetition, works beyond the pleasure principle. In his 1920 reflection on the subject, Freud indeed notes that the transference often brings back material that cannot have caused any pleasure. Thus, the actual status of displeasure and pain must be taken into account. In fact, if actual experience exists at all, the experience of pain is certainly an example:

> pain no doubt leaves permanent facilitations behind in ψ—as though there had been a stroke of lightning—facilitations which possibly do away with the resistance of the contact-barrier entirely…[162]

Any process of psychic elaboration stops short when pain occurs. This quasi-drive monopolizes all of the subject's attention. Speaking of pain and illness Freud writes,

> '[pain] concentrated his soul', says Wilhelm Busch of the poet suffering from toothache, 'in his molar's narrow hole.'[163]

---

161 de M'Uzan (1994).
162 Freud, (1895a), *SE* I, p. 307.
163 Freud (1914c), p. 82.

The Actual, Après-coup, and the Past

Impossible to repress or elaborate psychically, pain forces some humility upon the mind that might otherwise view itself as soaring above "lowly realities." Torturers know that by inflicting pain, they do not only harm the body. The psychic apparatus is what they seek to break. As long as pain persists, it is a one-blow-after-the-other sequence; repetition is absolute; there is no after-blow, no après-coup.[164] If a pure embodiment of the actual had to be found, pain would be the obvious choice. By focusing the entire range of libidinal cathexes on the very site of a breach in the psycho-biological dermis, pain is pure presence. One can distract oneself from pain when it is not too severe, but past a certain threshold of painful intensity, the psyche melts away, chronological time becomes everlasting, and the temporal perspective is abolished.

The analyst does not work at this level of intensity. As we know, analytic work cannot be done with urgency. For the work of differentiation between the soulical and the psychic to take place, a sufficiently large portion of the quantity of energy breaking-in must be immobilized and then bound by counter-investments. But this work never ceases, for it is impossible to eliminate the actual core that gives substance to the psychic by virtue of the link with the actuality of the body. Thus the "one-blow-after-the-other" of the actual does not stop, even when it is alleviated by a certain degree of psychic binding and by the differentiation of the agencies. When this blow-after-blow sequence, this pulsation, takes on crippling proportions, the kind of après-coup the transference can provide offers a way to transcend/preserve the actual within a process of psychic elaboration. The analyst's enigma, the seduction inherent in the analyzing situation, summons the perceptual complex again, but this time under conditions able to permit inclusion of the actual in the context of a psychic elaboration to which the *Nebenmensch*,

---

164 Translator's note: in French the word *coup*, translated here as "blow," appears also in the term *"après-coup"* (which, translated literally, would be "after-blow").

who is embodied by the analyst, may contribute thanks to a method grounded in ethics.

However, as Jacques André has stressed, one must take account of the fact that après-coup begins with a new edition of a painful a painful blow (*coup*):

> Après-coup is a trauma and if it is not simple repetition it is because it contains elements of signification which, provided they are met with a process of listening and interpretation, open the way to a modification of the past.[165]

André has drawn our attention to the fact that the familiar French expression "après-coup" (but the reasoning applies just as well to the English "deferred") might lead us to focus only on the retrospective aspect, to the resignification of the past, to rewriting:

> all things which are in no way psychoanalytic and which relate just as much to the hermeneuticist or the historian. [It is not only the traumatic dimension that would get lost,] but also the fact that the reality that breaches at the time of stage 1 is psychic, the blow (*coup*) that is dealt comes from within.[166]

To which I would add a two points. First of all, following what I have developed, the blow that is dealt does indeed come from within, but the distinction between actual and psychic urges me to suggest that this blow might be actual and not yet psychic. If there is a blow, a repetition, it is because it has not yet been transferred into the psychic and temporal domain. Corollary: it has not yet become past. Jacques André himself evokes subjects that are not inscribed in time. This leads me to propose, as my second point, a slight modification of the first quotation

---

165 André (2009), p. 1295.
166 *Op. cit.*, p. 1294.

from André: with the mechanism of après-coup, it is not a matter of *modifying* the past but of *instituting* it, based on the actual that is responsible for the blow. This is not merely a question of vocabulary; in the spirit as André's reflection, my point is to elucidate the mechanism and effects of après-coup. Modifying the past can be envisioned only if one acknowledges the fact that the "past" in question must be put in inverted commas, that it is not really past yet. How could that be the case anyway, as what is to be modified belongs to the supposedly atemporal unconscious? Such a "past" is so little past that it (re-)presents itself and still strikes blows! It is active in the present; it is present and atemporal at once: that is what the actual is. The "after" brought about by the "après-coup" will stem from the creation of an authentic past, the one which, once elaborated, will alleviate the actual pain of trauma.

Characters in Search of a Past

Luigi Pirandello's most famous play, *Six Characters in Search of an Author*[167] seems to me capable of illustrating my point. To some extent, any analysand could be said to be, in his or her way, a character in search of an author. Much like the six beleaguered beings who show up in a theater one day asking to be dramatized, patients consult an analyst when they cannot represent to themselves whatever "screw might be missing." Now, the missing screw is the twist in a story that has stalled, closing off the possibility of an open future and making loops instead; its outline has become entangled, knotted. The problem that arises is how to move from the unconscious thing, opaque and unyielding, that continues striking blows, to its psychic formalization, which is to say to its representation. This is the problem faced by the six characters in Pirandello's play. The theater's professional staff do not understand what prevents the six visitors from simply "acting" their

---

[167] I relied on this example in Scarfone (2012b) but had not yet distinguished between presentation, repetition, and (re-)presentation or between psychic and soulical. I am therefore including an excerpt from this text, though I have made a few changes.

drama. The Mother, for example, is opposed to it most energetically, and the theater manager fails to understand her refusal. He exclaims:

> "But since it has happened already, I'm sorry but… I don't understand!"

To which the Mother replies:

> "It's taking place now and always. My torment is not a finished one, sir! I am still alive and present, at each minute of this torment which is mine and which renews itself, ever alive and present."[168]

From a metapsychological perspective, the problem could not be better formulated. Whatever has not yet succeeded in getting itself *represented* continues happening and cannot rest. "Something took place and has no place"[169] and carries on repeating itself, perpetuating a torment which, though it does not always have the intensity of torture, can nonetheless cripple the psyche and impair a life. Pirandello himself, in a preface, highlights this very exchange, pointing out that the Mother is the only one in the play who does not really know she is a character. Concerning what she cries out to the manager, Pirandello writes:

> She *feels* it, without being conscious of it, and feels it therefore as something inexplicable: but she feels it so terribly that she doesn't think it can be something to explain either to herself or to others.[170]

---

[168] Pirandello (1977), p. 53 (my translation). Let us note that I modified the translation here: in two Italian versions I was able to consult, the Mother cries: "il mio strazio non è *finito*," but the French and the English translators seem to have read "non è *finto*" and thus translated the line as: "My torment isn't a pretended one" (*Op. cit.*, p. 53). Amazingly, in both cases, the statement is tenable, metapsychologically speaking, in that if the torment could be transformed into fiction, i.e., dramatized, it could become a thing of the past.
[169] Pontalis (1977), p. 197.
[170] Pirandello, Preface to *Six Characters in Search of an Author*, op. cit., pp. 21–23.

The Actual, Après-coup, and the Past

The Mother is like an unconscious—and therefore actual—imago, which the psyche fails to "explain to itself," to remember (i.e., to "remind to oneself" in the sense I discussed in relation to Freud's *Project*) or, in other words, which fails to "reproduce itself in the psychic domain". In the logic of Pirandello's play, I would say that the scene whose reproduction the Mother seeks to avoid is precisely not a representation, either theatrically speaking or psychologically speaking, but a *(re-)presentation*, a repetition in act, pregnant with all the pain of trauma.

Using Michel de M'Uzan's categories, this would be closer to repetition of the identical than to repetition of the same. It does not, however, consist in a repetition that is pure discharge; despite the Mother's reluctance, the characters wish to be dramatized; they want to step out of the impasse in which they find themselves, to free themselves from their unpast (*impassé*). They wish to be able *to put into the past* the hideous things that are haunting them. In such a process of putting into the past, like the one aimed at by the analytic work, or the repressed, the split off, even the foreclosed, patients (re-)present themselves in the actuality of the transference and, in this way, can live in the present, until, to borrow Augustine's words, they start becoming the past.

A play within a play, for us, the audience, the drama of *Six Characters* remains a representation and Pirandello had to rely on all his creative genius to give us at least some intuition of the *thing* which, embedded at the heart of this theatrical representation, (re-)presents itself and endows dramatic art with its power. Naturally, *any* theatrical play worthy of the name, like any authentic work of art, succeeds in conveying real presence through the artifice of the representation.[171] With *Six Characters in Search of an Author*, Pirandello nonetheless sought to go further, to shed full light on the non-scenic, actual side for which dramatic art usually provides

---

171 Gumbrecht (2003) has developed an inspiring reflection on this matter.

some form of scenic coating. In this sense, the play is a meta-theatrical, or even a metapsychological, reflection on the potentialities of theater. It also enlightens us regarding the difficult shift from actual to ordinary temporality. By showing us what tends to (re-)present to itself, having not yet achieved representation, the play foregrounds this intermediary mechanism which one could say, in *Six Characters*, consists of an actual moment endowed with great dramatic power. (Re-)presentation is a painful yet necessary moment; at first a form of resistance to elaboration, it can become elaboration's most reliable guide.

Repetition in the transference can sometimes appear to be very close to repetition of the identical; in those cases, it will then seem to lead the analysis in the direction of an impasse, but most of the time it turns out to be a repetition in the sense of a (re-)presentation in which case multiple re-occurrences can converge and elicit an interpretive act possible, making possible the effects of après-coup. So, between the two types of repetition noted by Pontalis—acting out as discharge and a transferential repetition potentially carrying meaning—there is good reason to insert what (re-)presents itself in the transference both as a repetition *and* as a rough form of representation. This pulls into the potential for analysis situations which, however extreme they seem at the time they are experienced, ultimately can find a way onto the psychic side. This intermediate level may be what Freud had in mind when he says, in the context of treatment, that acting out must be caught "*in statu nascendi.*"[172] This happens if the push toward action is not strong enough to prevent the initiation of binding. Freud later attributes the role of initiation of binding to the repetition compulsion conceived of as an attempt (successful in the fort/da game, but unsuccessful in traumatic neuroses) to bind the quantity of excitation that generated the trauma.

---

172 Freud (1914a), p. 193

As Jacques André writes, to result in a true symbolization, this rough form of representation requires of listening and interpretation. The locus of the transference is nowhere but within an intersubjective situation, and the analyst's availability to accommodate the transference can make all the difference. Except that listening and interpretation, which seem ordinary to the analyst, in certain borderline situations can be jeopardized by an "actuality" that fights off any attempt to ensnare it in meaning.

Beyond Interpretation

Because I have dealt at length with my treatment of Solange in an earlier paper,[173] I will not present the history of the case except to say that at a moment in the course of an analysis that, up until then, had been most satisfying, an intense transference developed leading us to an impasse. This became manifest in Solange a little before the long summer break, in the form of severe insomnia, as resistant to my interpretations as to the medication prescribed by her doctor. The insomnia had started shortly after I informed her of the dates of my holiday. An initial meaning I tried to ascribe to this symptom was that it aimed to make me worry about her while I was away, if not make me feel guilty for leaving her. This was probably not untrue, but communicating it to the patient had no effect whatever.

As one can imagine, the insomnia had serious consequences on Solange's health, but it was extremely detrimental also to her professional life as she had to read hundreds of pages of text on a daily basis; that soon became impossible. Consequently, the nearer we came to the summer break, the more intense became her anxiety about her sleeplessness, which generated a vicious circle. Also escalating was an anger that arose around the same time, an anger I had never seen in her before. It reached the point where she threatened to "break everything" in my consulting room if I did not do something to relieve

---

173 Scarfone (2006b), pp. 27–44.

her. I suggested intensifying our work before my break, seeing her every day of the week, which at first proved rather unfruitful. The sessions had become sterile displays of mood: only Solange's sleepless nights were on the agenda with no dreams or associations; her anger was gradually morphing into a rage that my interventions did not calm. This culminated during a session when, after lying on the couch, then standing up and pacing around the room, and crying and raising her voice, she lay down again and, sobbing, begged me to "do something." Having run out of any "analytic" means at my disposal, I said to her: "This is all I can do, but I will do it if it might relieve you." I then stretched out my arm and gently put my hand on her forehead. Solange calmed down, tears ran down her cheeks, and we remained like this in silence for a few minutes, until the end of the session, after which she left without a word. The following day she informed me that she had slept all night. In the few remaining sessions, the analysis resumed a more ordinary course and I was able to go on break, as relieved as she was. But I continue to mull over this transferential crisis and would like to bring my latest findings to bear on the episode.

In the article in which I first related this story, I outlined a few features of Solange's analysis that seemed to have led to the critical situation we experienced, including the emergence of a dangerous maternal imago clamping down on the libidinally charged relationship between Solange and her father. My conclusion in the article was that my appeasing gesture had substituted a tender form of maternal presence for the violent maternal imago (a devouring whale) that had presented itself in the course of the analysis. I still think there is some truth to this reading, but I also suggested that the very work of the analysis, in the most "classical" sense (provided the word means anything), had led to this "navel" of the treatment. In the context of the current discussion, I cannot help locating such a navel within stage 1 of the "actual," on the "soulical" plane, where language proves insufficient, where we arrive at a stratum of psychic aphasia, or better *in-fantia*.

The Actual, Après-coup, and the Past

In the context of my recent work,[174] I realized that the incident during which I placed my hand on Solange's forehead was in fact inscribed in a tangle much more complex than I imagined, and I was better able to understand how my gesture—which was not raw "acting out," but of whose unconscious roots I was nonetheless unaware—stemmed from a knot of the actual in my countertransference. I therefore must return to an aspect of Solange's history that now appears to me in a clearer light.

Solange's father had had one of his legs amputated some time before his death, which occurred when my patient was still a child. Noteworthy at this point is the fact that her father brought home a prosthesis, an artificial leg he never wore and that remained put away in a closet. More than once, Solange told me about her repeated visits to this closet and her contemplation, with mixed feelings, of this unsettling and fascinating "leg." What I could not tell Solange was that I had experienced something similar. When I visited my grandfather's house as a child, I would often go open a drawer surreptitiously in order to contemplate, shivering slightly, the prosthesis for the arm my grandfather had lost at the dreadful battle of Caporetto during World War I. Like Solange's father, my grandfather did not like to bother with this artificial limb, which only served an aesthetic purpose and had none of the functionalities of today's prostheses.

At the time, the similarity between our two stories seemed merely one of these coincidences that lead us to settle more willingly on analysands whose history includes, without our knowledge, something that resonates with our own. This is all I ever made of it until the day when, speaking about my grandfather and his missing arm, I saw myself stretching out my arm toward Solange's forehead in a desperate gesture. I then saw my gesture resurface like a dream, emerging from the mycelium of our two childhood tales, tied together, hinging on a "missing limb."

---

174 Scarfone (2012)

What was going on during those sessions when Solange was more and more unwell, and I was feeling more and more overwhelmed by the events, was a kind of amputation of my analytic function, a form of castration yielding a feeling of growing powerlessness as the date of my vacation drew near. The extension of my arm now appears to me as an "actual" solution, "actual" in the sense of "stage 2." To an actual crisis (in the first sense), an actual response (in the second sense) is given. Granted, my gesture was not symbolic at the outset, but it was a symbolizing gesture (in keeping with "symbolizing somatizations"[175]), overdetermined by our two infantile experiences charged with mystery and the uncanny.

Until the transference neurosis was established, one could say that Solange and I worked in an unconscious complicity. The patient "responded" to the work of the analysis in various ways: dreams, memories, the disappearance of symptoms, which naturally gave me the impression that all was going well. Today, I understand one of the effects of this positive transference to have been Solange's disinvestment of the paternal phallus and her transference of her desires onto the person of the analyst. However, the announcement of my vacation, just when she was at the peak of her transferential investment, amounted to telling her that, by leaving, I would deprive her of what she had deposited in me. I would go away, taking the phallus with me, leaving her bereft and alone, castrated and exposed to the threat of the phallic maternal imago that had recently arisen on the scene of her analysis, with no *fort/da* game through which she might symbolize my absence. Solange therefore reacted in the way I described, but it is worth noting that this reaction rendered us both powerless: by being completely insomniac, she would no longer have any dreams, memories, or associations; all that was left was a pressing demand that I "do something"; the psychic material was abraded, an "actual" urgency was all that remained, which plunged me, in turn, into a kind

---

175 Christophe Dejours (2001)

of paralysis, amputating my function as an analyst. This feeling of castration was alleviated by my gesture, as I now see it, in more than one way: (1) it restored my bodily integrity, which in the imaginary order had found itself missing a limb (via activation of the identification with my amputated grandfather); (2) it furnished Solange with the missing phallus, albeit with the mediation of an "upward displacement," as Freud would put it; (3) it gave her evidence of a wish to assuage her distress and allowed her to rekindle the experience of tender maternal care.

As I have written elsewhere, I do not propose my gesture as a "new technique." It is certainly possible that another analyst in my place would have found words performing the same positive effect as my gesture; words that would have had the quality and function of a gesture, as probably happens often in all analyses. The fact is that, in spite of all their theoretical and clinical skills, analysts face similar situations of impasse. In such impasses solutions must: 1) correspond to what the actual situation requires while remaining within the limits of ethically acceptable practice (not "anything goes"); 2) rest on the basis of the personal psychic complexion and be deeply rooted in the unconscious countertransference.

I report what happened to see what can be learned from an unplanned gesture that, as I see it, stopped this analysis from turning into a catastrophe. In the context of this paper, one could say that this is a case which, on one hand, confirms "the end of representation" and where what is (re-)presented takes an unexpected form, unexpected by both analysand and analyst. On the other hand, it illustrates resumption of movement from an actual impasse toward symbolization. Let us note that what can be held true regarding a gesture like mine applies just as much to interpretation itself. Commenting on one of Winnicott's famous interventions,[176] Gantheret writes:

---

[176] Winnicott (1971), in the chapter "Creativity and its Origins", p. 85-88.

The statement asserts itself spontaneously but it is only by virtue of an *act* which consists in the statement, through the intervention of some enactment which, on principle, is in contradiction with speaking: a contradiction which within the analytic method is a matter of principle; but a principle of which the interpretation is nonetheless a transgression.[177]

*

Another dimension of the incident which is worthy of mention is the fact that after uttering only a few words, as I stretched out my arm Solange and I remained silent. And as Josef Ludin writes, "few things make presence more present than silence!"[178] Could such silent presence, as much my silence as Solange's, have been like the gesture itself, what helped us to come unstuck from the painful actuality and to return the psyche to the side of representation? For Solange, did silence and motionlessness while for a few minutes my hand remained on her forehead constitute the opaque nucleus, the "thing" at the center of my enigmatic being, at the very moment that all sorts of images could provide it psychic coating (for example, experiencing it as a maternal hand checking a child for fever)?

For my part, I was aware that I was giving in to my patient's need and appeal that I "do something" and I was worried by the idea that had just created a precedent that would haunt us in the analysis for a long time. But that did not happen. I am now inclined to think that my gesture revived the "life of the soul" of the analytic chimera (de M'Uzan) which had been paralyzed. It therefore mobilized the embodied psyche on the basis of the primordial, soulical stratum that revealed itself in the actual mode via a stubborn case of insomnia that deprived us of dreams and other psychic productions. The insomnia

---

177 Winnicott (1971), in the chapter "Creativity and its Origins", p. 85-88.
178 Ludin (2009).

assumed the characteristics of a proper actual neurosis, the resistant core of Solange's transference neurosis. In this case, it is hardly surprising that one can see the analytic situation as a site of primal seduction (Laplanche) and the analytic session as an erogenous zone (de M'Uzan).[179]

The analytic scene was truly ablaze; representation had been seriously disrupted for a long time, to the point of coming to a halt, setting off in the analyst a function distinct from the interpretive one. Would it be an exaggeration to continue to think of the "situation," strictly speaking, as remaining an "analyzing situation?" It seems to me that similar incidents, of highly varying seriousness, are likely to occur in any analysis. These days, English-language publications abound with references to the concept of *enactment*, which refers to unintentional acting out by the analyst.[180]

Common Sense and the Untouchable

Another specificity of the scene with Solange is that it involved the sense of touch. Touch is a fundamental sensory modality from which all the other senses seem to stem. The senses of taste and smell depend on micro tactile exchanges between incoming molecules and receptors on the tongue, the palate, and the nasal mucous membrane. Hearing too is a matter of contact: sound waves stir up the air that hits the eardrum, leading it to set hammer and stirrup in motion sequentially. As for sight, Merleau-Ponty regards it as a variation of tactile palpation.[181] He quotes Herder, for whom "man is a perpetual *sensorium commune*, who is touched either on one side or on the other."[182] This "common sense" (not to be confused with "common opinion," to which the phrase generally refers) is a concept

---

179 Laplanche (1991); de M'Uzan (2006).
180 See Bohleber, Fonagy et al. (2013).
181 Merleau-Ponty (1968 [1964]), p. 133.
182 Merleau-Ponty (2012 [1945]), p. 248.

that has been developed since antiquity in philosophical and medical texts. In an outstanding book,[193] Daniel Heller-Roazen carries out an historical and epistemological survey of the concept, suggesting that the *sensus communis* that thinkers have invoked throughout the centuries might well amount to the sense of touch, inasmuch as it relates to what Merleau-Ponty (whom Heller-Roazen quotes extensively) refers to as *the untouchable*:

> To touch and to touch oneself (to touch oneself = touched-touching). They do not coincide in the body: the touching is never exactly the touched. This does not mean that they coincide 'in the mind' or at the level of 'consciousness'. Something else than the body is needed for the junction to be made: it is made in *the untouchable*. That of the other which I will never touch. But what I will never touch, he does not touch either, there is no privilege of the self over the other here, therefore consciousness is not the untouchable.[184]

Immediately after this, Merleau-Ponty mentions the unconscious, in a parallel that to me seems to me most appropriate when I try to reflect on the touching of Solange's forehead episode:

> The untouchable is not a touchable that happens to be inaccessible—the unconscious is not a representation that is in fact inaccessible. The negative here is not *a positive that is elsewhere* (a transcendent)——It is a true negative ... an original of the *elsewhere*, a *Selbst* that is an Other, a Hollow.[185]

In Merleau-Ponty's phenomenology and in his notion of the *flesh*, I believe I can see an opening through which to better understand

---

183 Heller-Roazen (2007).
184 Merleau-Ponty (1968 [1964]) *op. cit.*, p. 254. Translation modified
185 *Ibid.* Translation modified

the soothing effect of my touch when as an analyst nothing else was within my reach. As we saw, this pitiful gesture expressed an attempt to reach Solange in the solitude of her distress, an attempt that also revealed my own distress and my feeling of being completely alone, without a clue on how to go about it, in having to face a situation both urgent and unprecedented. Might we think, following Merleau-Ponty, that what occurred within what my touch expressed was in fact the activation of "true negativity", with the possibility of reopening the channels of communication between the *thing* and its predicates, between the *actual* and the *psychic*, instead of leaving Solange mired in an "actual neurosis" that had been resumed in the transference? Or, conversely, am I striving at all costs to find some good in my desperate gesture when I underline the ensuing resumption of the analytic process? The outcome of the transferential crisis definitely leads me to suppose that, through the apparent positivity of an act, some "work of the negative," to borrow André Green's phrase, managed to sidle in all the same.[186] In the chapter "Hegel and Freud" in *The Work of the Negative*, Green writes, in the same vein as Merleau-Ponty:

> One must understand that the status of the negative presents the particularity of being at once the other side of the positive, connoting a type of valency contrary to what is being affirmed initially, *but it is also the revelation of a being that is radically different in nature from the positive*, so that approaching the latter by the means which are appropriate to it will never disclose its true nature.[187]

In my view, the *untouchable* seems to correspond to what is radically other and to be similar to the other negative figures I have tried to define such as the *unpast* and, more generally, the *actual*.

---

186 Green (1999 [1993])
187 *Op. cit.*, p. 36.

Perhaps it is not by chance that the example I chose, in the opening pages of this essay, to illustrate the concept is that of an oculus, a hollow. Despite its apparent positivity, the actual requires, in order to characterize it, that we speak of what it lacks, psychic coating in particular. In this sense, the aspect of its "presentation" cannot be apprehended positively; what presents itself is on the order of the "thing" and all it can generate is anxiety, unless it acquires representable attributes by what I call, slightly modifying Rolland's notion, the (re-)presentation compulsion.

Ethics and the Knowledge of the Unconscious

It is important to be clear that the "true negative," the hollow, and the untouchable are not metaphysical entities but depend on a fundamental disposition that, in the first place, is required of the analyst. This is what I referred to, following Lyotard, as *passibility* at the beginning of my discussion, another word to denote a self-imposed form of *passivity*. But let us not be wary of words, especially not of the word passivity, considering that psychoanalysis leads us to encounter the word and the thing at the roots of what we do. First, the passivity of the *infans* in the fundamental anthropological situation, in consequence of being exposed to an "excess of message" on the part of the other, of the *Nebenmensch*. Active and helpful, this fellow human nonetheless generates, through the compromised messages, the experience within the *infans* of an inability to translate, an inability to understand: a contact with the *thing* in the perceptual complex. Secondly, the passivity that the fundamental rule invites us to embrace, so that the experience of being decentered is not a mere relocation of the center in the other but a radical decentering in which, for a time, analysand and analyst become "a-centered". In practice this requires temporarily giving a vacation to the internal narrator who continually restores to the form of a familiar story whatever the work of the analysis brings forward, instead of letting the characters in search of an author (re-) present themselves and experience their drama in all its actuality; instead of letting them "perform" until the elements thus activated do not so much find a place that some prescience reserved for them but rather disrupt the scene, extend it, and raise it to a new and unexpected level.

While the incident I have reported from Solange's analysis is not put forward as an example to be emulated, it remains instructive. If it is, as I believe, a highly magnified version of myriads of little incidents of the same kind that occur in every analysis, it belongs in the series of inevitable failures of the psyche, periods of emptiness that reveal the soulical sphere, just as the back of a painting reveals the wooden framework of the canvas, the actual framework in the first sense of actual, but likely to be rehabilitated by the artist, thus endowing the work with more actuality. I am thinking here of the framework of the canvas represented in Velazquez's *Las Meninas*, an often discussed work of art,[188] in which the inclusion of the back of the canvas in the painting, combined with other elements, lends a remarkable presence to the whole. A painting in a painting with Velazquez, a play in a play with Pirandello: yet in neither case is there any *mise-en-abyme*, any infinite regress; on the contrary, the actual supplies a safety-catch, an anchoring point (*point de capiton*) for the representation that then seems addressed to us.

Actual moments, big or small, occur quite often and ensure that no one is ever in analysis during an entire session. How then can on one resume the analysis and the working through? In the text that addresses this question, Freud does not answer it but implies that all analysts know the answer. Winnicott does the same in his text on "The Use of an Object": toward the end of the article, where we would expect him to disclose, at last, what using an object (especially the analyst) might imply, he asserts simply that any analyst knows

---

188 It was discussed by Michel Foucault (1966), among others.

what it is like. In a discussion of these two examples,[189] I argued that Freud and Winnicott are in perfect agreement: we cannot describe in positive terms what or how to work through, or how to use the analyst, without thwarting these very processes. This is because what we analysts describe can quickly morph into what we *prescribe*, thus impeding the analysand's autonomy and creativity. This is one of the ways I understand the other necessary prescription that Laplanche formulates regarding the analyst's refusals: above all the refusal to know applied to oneself.

Such a refusal characterizes another form of self-imposed passivity: agreeing to hear without rushing to understand; refusing oneself comprehension so as to possibly open the passage to the "unheard of". In Solange's case, my failure to understand was inadvertent. However, I now believe that the noisy crisis we underwent took the place of a blatant need to touch something unfathomable, because that is the *thing* that, as an untranslatable residue, underlies the numerous layers of successive understandings.

I have said that certain refusals are prescribed for the analyst, yet no prescription can work without a basis that ensures its applicability. The refusal to understand, the analyst's self-imposed passivity, as well as the passivity demanded from the ego of the analysand, are justified because they are predicated on a radical passivity, "more passive still than any receptivity."[190] Here I am relying on the work of Emmanuel Levinas, who, though he does not often address psychoanalysis, is all the more interesting to us for having drawn a definitive border for the domain in which our discipline applies, though not out of a deliberate project to be in harmony with Freud.[191] Levinas's philosophical thought includes a reflection on

---

189 I drew this parallel between Freud and Winnicott in Scarfone (2004), pp. 109–123; reprinted in Scarfone (2012).
190 E. Levinas (1991 [1978]), p. 48.
191 Viviane Chétrit-Vatine (2012) has recently published a dissertation precisely on Levinas's thought in relation to psychoanalysis.

ethics that is well suited to guide us in the face of the failures of the psyche—when the theater is ablaze.

On such occasions we are ejected from our listening and interpretive position, we are summoned to remember that the analysand is the Other and that this Other besieges us, persecutes us, holds us hostage. This is no "persecutory delusion," but a persecution whose inevitability stems from the fact that the primary relation with this Other is based on an ethics of responsibility. Consequently, it is an ethics that is not added on to our practice as a code of deontology might be, rather this ethics is itself the condition for our access to any possible knowledge of the unconscious. Giving ourselves up as hostages of transference might be what lets something of the unconscious present itself to our ears. Our ethics is also our epistemology

The passivity evoked by Levinas is thus "more passive than any receptivity" because we are not *asked* to be passive or receptive. We *discover* ourselves immersed in this fundamental passivity, which we can either embrace or refuse. Is it not true, then, that when the analyst surrenders to the "grip" of transference, he implicitly accepts, whether he knows it or not, the status of hostage that, initially, has nothing to do with any technique or method? On the contrary, analytic technique and method are possible only insofar as they rest on this original passivity. The prescription of refusal suggested to analysts is thus no arbitrary coercion; rather, it the continuation of the basic condition of our work in the form of a self-imposed practice. Our egocentric perspective on the world drives us to deny, repress, circumvent this fact, or alternatively, to embellish it as a generous and imaginative offer made to the other in the context of a purely consensual exchange. Yet, while engaging in this exchange implies a contract and a mutuality, it remains true that there is nothing in it that is artificial or purely "theatrical" in the sense of "role-playing." We suspected as much in view of Freud's account of transference as a fire in a theater. Levinas teaches us that the theater itself is but one possible version of our life as besieged beings, but one that does not exempt us from our responsibility. What Pirandello shows in his play is what any good theatrical work brings into play, however implicitly. So much so that when Shakespeare tells us the world is a stage, he brings us no consolation: on this stage of the world, we embody a character, yet this does not lighten the actual burden of pain, of the incomprehensible *thing*-tale. A tale "full of sound and fury, signifying nothing" that we must endow with a psychic coating so that we turn it into a narrative, an outlook, a viable personal theory.

BIBLIOGRAPHY

Abraham, N. and Torok, M. (1994 [1978]) *The Shell and the Kernel*. Trans. N. Rand. Chicago: Chicago Univ. Press.

André J. (2009) "L'événement et la temporalité." *Revue française de psychanalyse*, vol. LXXIII, no. 5.

— et al. (2012) *Comprendre en psychanalyse*. Paris: PUF, Petite bibliothèque de psychanalyse.

Anzieu, D. (1989 [1985]) *The Skin Ego*. Trans. C. Turner, New Haven: Yale Univ. Press.

Arasse D. (1999) *L'Annonciation italienne*. Paris: Hazan.

Arendt, H. (1978) *The Life of the Mind*. San Diego: Harcourt Brace & Co.

— (1996 [1970]) *Considérations morales*, Paris: Rivages.

Aulagnier, P. (2001 [1975]) The Violence of Interpretation, Tr. A. Sheridan, Hove: Brunner-Routledge.

— (1989) "Se construire un passé, exposé théorique." *Journal de la psychanalyse de l'enfant*, no. 7, Bayard Éditions.

Biche J.M. (1998) "Du chaos, de la temporalité et de la métapsychologie, entre autres." *Trans*, n° 9, "L'artefact," p. 131. http://mapageweb.umontreal.ca/scarfond/T9/9-Biche.pdf

Bohleber, W., Fonagy, P. et al. (2013) "Towards a Better Use of Psychoanalytic Concepts: A Model Using the Concept of Enactment." *International Journal of Psychoanalysis*, vol. 94, no. 3, pp. 501-30.

Borges, J. L. *Otras inquisiciones*. Madrid, Spain: Alianza Editorial, 1993.

Botella, C. & Botella, S. (2015) *The Work of Psychic Figurability: Mental States Without Representation*, Hove (East Sussex): Brunner-Routledge, The New Library of Psychoanalysis.

Bourguignon, A. et al. (1989) *Traduire Freud*, Paris: PUF.

Butler, J. (2005), *Giving an Account of Oneself*, New York, NY: Fordham University Press.

Castoriadis-Aulagnier, P. (2001 [1975]) *The Violence of Interpretation*. Trans. A. Sheridan, Hove (East Sussex): Brunner-Routledge.

Chétrit-Vatine, V. (2012) *The Ethical Seduction of the Analytic Situation*. Trans. A. Weller, London: Karnac Books.

Coblence, F. (2005) *Les attraits du visible*, Paris: PUF, Petite bibliothèque de psychanalyse.

— (2010) "La vie d'âme. Psyché est corporelle." *Rev. Française de psychanalyse*, vol. LXXIV, n°5.

Dejours, C. (2001) *Le corps d'abord*, Paris: Payot.

Derrida, J. (1978 [1967]) "Freud and the Scene of Writing," in *Writing and Difference*. Chicago: Chicago Univ. Press.

Donnet J.-L. (2001) "De la règle fondamentale à la situation analysante," *Revue française de psychanalyse*, vol. LXV, no. 1, pp. 243-257.

— (2009) *The Analyzing Situation*. Trans. A. Weller, London: Karnac Books.

Edelman, G. (1989) *The remembered present: A biological theory of consciousness*. New York: Basic Books.

Ferenczi, S. (1949 [1932]) Confusion of the Tongues between the Adults and the Child, *International Journal of Psychoanalysis*, 30: 225-230.

Foucault, M. (1970 [1966]) *The Order of Things*. New York: Pantheon Books.

Freud, S. (1891) *On Aphasia*. London and New York: Imago Publishing, 1953.

— (1895a) *Project for a Scientific Psychology*, SE I.

— (1895b) The Psychotherapy of Hysteria, *Studies on Hysteria*, SE II.

— (1896a) Letter on 22 February 1896, *The Complete Letters of Sigmund Freud to Wilhelm Fliess, 1887-1904*. Cambridge: Harvard UP.

— (1896b) "Further Remarks on the Neuro-Psychoses of Defence". SE III.

— (1897) Letter on 21 September 1897, *The Complete Letters of Sigmund Freud to Wilhelm Fliess, 1887-1904*, Op. cit.

— (1898a) The Psychical Mechanisms of Forgetfulness, SE III, 297-300.

— (1898b) Sexuality in the aetiology of the neuroses, SE III.

— (1899) Screen memories, SE III.

— (1900) *The Interpretation of Dreams*, SE IV and V.

— (1905a [1901]), Fragment of an Analysis of a Case of Hysteria, SE VII.

— (1905b) *Three Essays on the Theory of Sexuality*, SE VII.

— (1908) Hysterical Phantasies and their Relation to Bisexuality, SE IX.

Bibliography

— (1912) The Dynamics of Transference, *SE* XII

— (1914a) Remembering, Repeating and Working-Through, *SE* XII.

— (1914b) Observations on Transference-Love, *SE* XII.

— (1914c) On Narcissism: An Inttroduction, *SE* XIV.

— (1915a) Instincts and their Vicissitudes, *SE* XIV.

— (1915b) Repression, *SE* XIV.

— (1915c) "The unconscious," *SE* XIV.

— (1915-17) *Introductory Lectures on Psycho-Analysis*, *SE* XV.

— (1920) *Beyond the Pleasure Principle*, *SE* XVIII.

— (1924) *The Ego and the Id*, *SE* XIX.

— (1925a [1924]) A Note Upon the 'Mystic Writing-Pad', *SE* XIX.

— (1925b) Negation, *SE* XIX.

— (1930), *Civilization and its Discontents*, *SE* XXI

— (1932) Lecture XXXI: The Dissection of the Psychical Personality, *New Introductory Lectures on Psycho-Analysis*, *SE* XXII. ("Die Zerlegung der psychischen Persönlichkeit," in *Gesammelte Werke*, Vol. 15, pp. 62–86. Frankfurt: Fischer Taschenbuch Verlag.)

— (1933) *New Introductory Lectures on Psycho-Analysis*, *SE* XXII.

— (1937a) *Analysis Terminable and Interminable*, S.E. XXIII.

— (1937b) *Constructions in Analysis* S.E. XXIII.

— (1938) *An Outline of Psycho-Analysis*, *SE* XXIII.

— (1985) *The Complete Letters of Sigmund Freud to Wilhelm Fliess*, ed. J. Masson. Cambridge, MA: Harvard Univ. Press.

Freud, S. & Breuer, J. (1895) *Studies on Hysteria*, *SE* II.

Gagnebin, M & de Milly, J. (ed.) (2012) *Michel de M'Uzan ou le saisissement créateur*, Paris: Champ-Vallon, Coll. L'or de l'Atalante.

Gantheret, F. (1990) "Une forme de temps," *Nouvelle revue de psychanalyse*, n° 41, "L'épreuve du temps."

— (1998) "Traces et chair," in *Moi, monde, mots*, Paris, Gallimard.

— (2013) *Les multiples visages de l'Un. Le charme totalitaire*. Paris: PUF, Petite bibliothèque de psychanalyse.

Gopnik, A. & Meltzoff, A. N. (1997) *Words, Thoughts, and Theories*. Cambridge, MA: MIT Press.

Green, A. (1972) "*De l'Esquisse à L'interprétation des rêves: coupure et clôture*," Nouvelle revue de psychanalyse, n° 5 "L'espace du rêve", pp. 155-180.

— (1999 [1993]) *The Work of the Negative*. London: Free Association Books.

— (2002 [2000]) *Time in Psychoanalysis: Some Contradictory Aspects*. Trans. A. Weller. London: Free Association Books.

Guenancia, P. (2009) *Le regard de la pensée. Philosophie de la représentation*. Paris: PUF, "Fondements de la politique."

Gumbrecht, H.U. (2003) *Production of Presence: What Meaning Cannot Convey*, Redwood City: Stanford Univ. Press.

Heller-Roazen, D. (2007) *The Inner Touch. Archaeology of a Sensation*. Brooklyn: Zone Books.

Imbeault, J. (1997) *Mouvements*, Paris: Gallimard.

— (2000) "Petit et grand infantile," *Le fait de l'analyse*, n° 8, "La maladie sexuelle", pp. 23-43.

Jullien, F. (2012) *Cinq concepts proposés à la psychanalyse*, Paris: Grasset.

Kahn, L. (1993) "La petite maison de l'âme," in *La petite maison de l'âme*, Paris: Gallimard, pp. 33-54.

— (2012), L'écoute de l'analyste. *De l'acte à la forme*, Paris: PUF, Le fil rouge.

Klein, E. (2005 [2004]) *Chronos: How Time Shapes our Universe*. Thunder's Mouth Press.

Lacan, J. (2006 [1954]) "Response to Jean Hyppolite's Commentary on Freud's '*Verneinung*'," in *Écrits: The First Complete Edition in English*. Trans. B. Fink, New York: Norton.

— (1997a [1955]) *The Seminar of Jacques Lacan: The Psychoses* (Book III). Trans. R. Grigg. New York: Norton.

— (1997b [1960]) *The Seminar of Jacques Lacan: The Ethics of Psychoanalysis* (Book VII). Trans. D. Porter. New York: Norton.

— (1966) "La direction de la cure et les principes en son pouvoir." In *Écrits*. Paris: Seuil.

Bibliography

Lakoff, G. & Johnson, M. (1999) *Philosophy in the Flesh: The Embodied Mind and Its Challenge to Western Thought*. New York: Basic Books.

Lalande, A. (1988 [1926]) *Vocabulaire de la philosophie* (16th ed.). Paris: PUF.

Laplanche, J. (1976 [1970]), *Life and Death in Psychoanalysis*. Trans. J. Mehlman, Baltimore: The Johns Hopkins University Press.

— (1980) *Problématiques I. L'Angoisse*, Paris: PUF.

— (1989 [1987]) *New Foundations for Psychoanalysis*, trans. D. Macey, Oxford: Basil Blackwell. (*Nouveaux fondements pour la psychanalyse*. Paris: PUF.)

— (1992) "Notes on afterwardsness." In *Seduction, Translation, Drives*, ed. J. Fletcher & M. Stanton. London: ICA.

— (1999 [1991]) "Transference: Its Provocation by the Analyst". Trans. L. Thurston in *Essays on Otherness*. London: Routledge, p. 214-233.

— (1999 [1999a]) 'Seduction, Persecution, Revelation', Tr. J. Mehlman, in *Between Seduction and Inspiration: Man*, New York, The Unconscious in Translation.

— (1999 [1991b]) 'Time and the Other', Tr. L. Thurston, in *Essays on Otherness*, London: Routledge.

— (2015 [1999b]) 'Psychoanalysis as Antihermeneutics'. Tr. J. Mehlman, in *Between Seduction and Inspiration: Man*, New York, The Unconscious in Translation.

— (2011 [2006]). *Freud and the Sexual: Essays 2000-2006*. New York, The Unconscious in Translation.

— (2015 [1993]) *The Temptation of Biology: Freud's Theories of Sexuality*. Transl. Donald Nicholson-Smith. New York, The Unconscious in Translation.

Leclaire, M. & Scarfone, D. (2000) "Vers une conception unitaire de l'épreuve de réalité," *Revue française de psychanalyse*, vol. LXX, no. 3, pp. 885-912.

— (2004) Épreuve de réalité et jeu, *Revue française de psychanalyse*, vol. LXVIII, no. 1, pp. 19-37.

Levinas, E. (1985 [1982]) *Ethics and Infinity*, Tr. R. A. Cohen, Pittsburgh: Duquesne U. P.

— (1990 [1948]) *Time and the Other*. Tr. R. Cohen. Pittsburgh: Duquesne Univ. Press.

— (1991 [1978]) *Otherwise than Being, or, Beyond Essence*, Trans. A. Lingis, Dodrecht: Kluwer Academic Publishers.

— (1992) *Éthique comme philosophie première*, Paris: Rivages.

— (2003 [1971]) *Totalité et infini. Essai sur l'extériorité*. Paris: Le livre de poche.

Loewald, H. (2000 [1973]) "Some considerations on repetition and repetition compulsion," in *The Essential Loewald: Collected papers and monographs*. Hagerstown, MD: University Publishing Group, pp. 87–101.

Ludin, J. (2009), Au-delà du sens: la présence comme fondement du transfert, *Tribune psychanalytique*, vol. 9, "Présences."

Lyotard J.-F. (1988) *The Differend: Phrases in Dispute*, trans. G. Van Den Abbeele. Minneapolis, MN: Univ. of Minnesota Press.

— (1991a) *Lectures d'enfance*, Paris: Galilée.

— (1991b [1988]). *The Inhuman: Reflections of Time*. Stanford, Standford UP.

— (2000) ' La phrase-affect. D'un supplément au Différend' in *Misère de la philosophie*, Paris: Galilée.

— (2002 [2000]) "Emma," in *Philosophy, Politics, and the Sublime*, ed. H. J. Silverman. New York/London: Routledge. (*Misère de la philosophie*. Paris: Galilée.)

Merleau-Ponty, M. (2012 [1945]) *Phenomenology of Perception*. Trans. D. Landes. New York: Routledge. (*Phénoménologie de la perception*. Paris: Gallimard.)

— (1968 [1964]) *The Visible and the Invisible*, Transl. by A. Lingis, Evanston, Northwestern University Press.

Modell, A. (1990) *Other Times, Other Realities: Towards a Theory of Psychoanalytic Treatment*. Cambridge, MA: Harvard Univ. Press.

M'Uzan, M. de. (2004) *Aux confins de l'identité*, Paris: Gallimard, Connaissance de l'inconscient.

— (1996) *La bouche de l'inconscient*, Paris: Gallimard, Connaissance de l'inconscient.

— (1998 [1974]) Le processus psychanalytique et la notion de passé, in F. Duparc (ed.), *L'art du psychanalyste. Autour de l'œuvre de Michel de M'Uzan*, Lausanne: Delachaux & Niestlé.

— (2007 [1970]) "The Same and the Identical", trans. R. Simpson, *Psychoanalytic Quarterly* 76, pp. 1195-1205. ("Le même et l'identique," in *De l'Art à la Mort*. Paris: Gallimard.)

— (1968 [1964]) *The Visible and the Invisible*. Evanston: Northwestern UP.

Peirce, C.S. (1894) What is a sign?, in *The Essential Peirce*, Vol. 2 (1893-1913), (Edited by the Peirce Edition Project) Bloomington, Indiana University Press, 1998, pp. 4-10.

Pirandello, L. (2002 [1977]) *Six Characters in Search of an Author*, London: Nick Hern Books.

Pontalis J.-B. (1968) Question de mots in *Après Freud*, Paris: Gallimard.

— (1974) Bornes ou confins?, *Nouvelle revue de psychanalyse*, no. 10, "Aux limites de l'analysable", pp. 5-16.

— (1977) *Entre le rêve et la douleur*, Paris, Gallimard, Coll. Tel.

— (1990), *La force d'attraction*, Paris: Le Seuil, Bibliothèque du XXe Siècle.

— (1997a [1994]) "La saison de la psychanalyse," *Trans*, no. 4 (http://mapageweb.umontreal.ca/scarfond/T4/4-Pontalis.pdf). Reprinted in: *Ce temps qui ne passe pas*, Paris: Gallimard.

— (1997b) *Ce temps qui ne passe pas*. Paris: Gallimard.

Pragier, G. and Faure-Pragier, S. (2007) *Repenser la psychanalyse avec les sciences*, Paris: PUF.

Renik, O. (1999) "Getting real in analysis," in *Journal of Analytical Psychology*, 44(2), pp. 167–187.

— (2004) "Intersubjectivity in Psychoanalysis", Int J Psychoanal 85:1053–64.

Rolland J.-C. (2000) "La loi de Lavoisier s'applique à la matière psychique," *Libres cahiers pour la psychanalyse*, n° 2, «Dire non», pp. 19-36.

— (1998) *Guérir du mal d'aimer*, Paris, Gallimard, "Tracés."

Roussillon, R. (1991) "Épreuve 'd'actualité' et épreuve 'de réalité' dans le face-à-face 'psychanalytique'," *Revue française de psychanalyse*, vol. LV, 3, pp. 581-595.

Saint Augustine (1961) *Confessions*. London: Penguin Books (*Les Confessions*. Paris: Garnier Flammarion, 1964.)

Scarfone, D. (2002[2000]) Sexual and Actual, trans. Susan Fairfield, in Widlöcher et al. *Infantile Sexuality and Attachment*, London: Karnac.

— (2002) "Accuser reception." *Libres cahiers pour la psychanalyse*. No. 6 ("Les secrets de la seduction"), automne, pp. 67-80.

— (2003) "'It was not my mother': from seduction to negation." *New Formations*, 48:69-76.

— (2004) "À quoi œuvre l'analyse," *Libres cahiers pour la psychanalyse*, n°9, pp. 109-123, republished in Quartiers aux rues sans nom.

— (2006a) A Matter of Time. Actual Time and the Production of the Past, *Psychoana-*

lytic Quarterly, vol. LXXV, pp. 807-833.

— (2006b) Suite lunaire, *Penser/Rêver*, n° 9 "La double vie des mères", pp. 27-44, republished in *Quartiers aux rues sans nom*, op. cit. pp. 19-41.

— (2011 [2007]), Repetition : Between presence and Meaning, *Canadian Journal of Psychoanalysis/Revue canadienne de psychanalyse*, vol. 19, no. 1, Spring 2011, pp. 70-86.

— (2008) La séance d'analyse, ouverture de différends, in Corinne Enaudeau et al. (ed.) *Les transformateurs Lyotard*, Paris, Sens&Tonka, pp. 247-260.

— (2011a) Live Wires: When is the analyst at work?, *International Journal of Psychoanalysis*, vol. 92 pp.755–759.

— (2011b) "In the Hollow of Transference: The Analyst Between Activity and Passivity", trans. Dorothée Bonnigal-Katz. *Sitegeist, a Journal of Psychoanalysis and Philosophy* 4, Spring 2010, pp. 7-20.

— (2012a) *Quartiers aux rues sans nom*, Paris: Éditions de l'Olivier, coll. "Penser/rêver".

— (2012b) "Moments de grâce: présence et élaboration de l'impassé" in M.Gagnebin, and J. de Milly, pp. 31-41.

— (2013) From traces to signs, in H. B. Levine, G. Reed and D. Scarfone (ed.) *Unrepresented states and the construction of meaning*, London: Karnac Books.

(1999) *Webster's New World College Dictionary*, Fourth Edition. New York: Macmillan.

Weil, S. (1999 [1943]) "L'enracinement," in *Oeuvres*. Paris: Gallimard.

Widlöcher et al. (2002 [2000]) *Infantile Sexuality and Attachment*, Transl. Susan Fairfield, New York: Other Press.

Winnicott, D.W. (1989 [1964]) "Fear of Breakdown," in *Psychoanalytic Explorations*, Cambridge, MA: Harvard Univ. Press.

— (1971) *Playing and Reality*, New York: Penguin Books.

Zaltzman, N. (1997) "La pulsion anarchiste," in *La guérison psychanalytique*, Paris: PUF, coll. Épitres.

Index

activity, iv, 34, 49, 53, 57, 62, 88, 98, 125, 143, 180
afterwardsness, 177, 181
alterity, 67
analytic situation, 37, 41, 51, 57, 61, 130, 150, 165, 173
anlehnung, 181
après-coup, 34, 70, 78, 122, 138, 141, 143, 145, 149, 151-155, 157-159, 161, 163, 165, 167, 169, 171, 181-184
Aristophanes, 181

binding, 10, 31, 36-37, 43, 97, 105, 126, 153, 158
biology, 177

castration, 162-163, 181
condensation, 38-39, 94
criticism, 18, 62
culture, 34

death, 9-10, 48, 72, 88, 126, 146, 161
death drive, 10, 48, 182
decentering, 55, 108, 168
deferred action, 9, 182
delusion, 55, 171
Derrida, 82
determinism, 182
detranslation, 56, 184
displacement, 38-39, 42, 58, 94, 98, 137, 150, 163
Dora, 83, 87-88
dream-work, 94-95, 99, 103, 116
drive, 10, 45, 48, 69, 79, 112-113, 126-128, 146, 152

ego, 2, 4, 6, 18, 20, 34-35, 44, 47, 58-61, 63, 69, 74-76, 79-83, 86, 104-106, 125, 128-132, 170
enigma, 17, 43, 53, 56, 58-61, 63, 66-67, 92, 148, 153
erogenous zones, 182
Eros, 48, 135, 182
étrangèreté, 74
exigency, 181-182

fantasy, 23, 39, 47, 55-56, 88, 98, 120, 122, 130
filled-in transference, 42, 151
formation, 27, 87-88, 90, 120
Fundamental Anthropological Situation, 18, 54, 60-61, 66, 112-113, 168

General Theory of Seduction, 54, 109
goals, 2, 79, 129-130

Hegel, 123, 167
hollowed-out transference, 148

id, 2, 35, 47, 79, 137, 175, 182
infans, 14, 54, 59-60, 64, 90-91, 110-111, 113, 130, 168
infantile, 59, 66, 69, 76, 109-113, 162
infantile sexual theories, 110
inscription, 4
instinct, 115

leaning-on, 115
Levinas, x, 53-55, 57-62, 66-67, 74, 108, 170-171

metaphor, viii, 2, 4, 29, 97, 140-141, 143, 145
metaphysical, ix, 168, 183
metapsychological, 31-32, 34, 40, 50-51, 78, 80, 91, 105, 111, 137, 156, 158
metonymy, 17
mother, 17-18, 21, 25-27, 43, 91, 102-104, 115-117, 156-157
mourning, 36, 57

narcissism, 48, 115
nature, 3, 14, 18, 45, 87, 167

oceanic feeling, 104

passivity, iv, 53-54, 56-60, 62-64, 66-67, 76, 129-130, 168, 170-171
penis, 59
perception, 4, 7, 49, 69, 80-82, 84, 89, 91, 95-96, 104-106, 113, 121-122

phylogenesis, 109-110, 183
Poincaré, 151
primal scene, 26, 59-60, 102
provocation, 53, 56, 62

recentering, 55-56
repetition compulsion, 5, 9-10, 32, 47, 97, 119, 158
residues, 5, 83, 90, 108, 113, 121
resistance, 1, 33, 45, 50-51, 59-60, 73, 86, 131, 152, 158
responsibility, 65, 171-172
retroactive, 46, 122, 141
return of the repressed, viii, 85
revelation, 167

Schreber, 55
seduction, 17-18, 25, 47, 54-57, 60, 62, 64, 66-67, 69, 102, 108-110, 112, 153, 165
seele, 142, 144, 146
self-preservative instincts, 115
semiology, 99
slips of the tongue, 39, 102-103
soul, 1, 35, 40, 49, 75-76, 106, 109, 112-113, 126-128, 134, 140-146, 152, 164
stranger, 74

strangerness, 74, 86, 92
structural model, 4
sublimation, 75
symptoms, 83, 85, 87-88, 107, 162

temporality, 11, 14, 16, 20, 24, 28, 109, 112, 120, 128, 132, 138, 140, 143-146, 149, 158
temptation, ix, 108, 177
tendencies, 130
timeless, vii, ix, 3, 5-6, 18, 21-22, 27-28, 45, 135
topography, viii-ix, 4, 142
transcendence, 59, 73
transference, iv-v, ix-x, 24, 27, 31-32, 37, 40-44, 46, 51, 53, 55-59, 61-63, 65-67, 70, 76, 78, 100, 104, 119, 121-122, 133-134, 137, 147-153, 157-159, 162, 165, 167, 171
translation, iii-iv, vii-viii, 7-9, 11, 14, 17-20, 22, 24, 31, 41-42, 54, 56, 62, 65-66, 69, 86, 88, 90, 95-96, 99, 107, 110, 113, 117, 121, 124, 126, 132, 135-137, 142, 146, 156, 166

unbinding, 7, 10, 36-37, 43, 57

Dominique Scarfone MD (author) is full professor at the Department of Psychology of the *Université de Montréal* where he teaches psychoanalytic theory, does clinical supervision, and conducts research. A psychoanalyst in private practice, he is a member of the *Société* and of the *Institut psychanalytique de Montréal (Canadian Psychoanalytic Society and Institute)*. He was associate editor of the *International Journal of Psychoanalysis* and is on the editorial board of the *Psychoanalytic Quarterly*. He has published four books: *Jean Laplanche* (Eng. transl. *Laplanche: An introduction*), *Oublier Freud? Mémoire pour la psychanalyse*, *Les Pulsions*, and *Quartiers aux rues sans nom*. He co-edited *Unrepresented States and the Construction of Meaning*, with Howard Levine and Gail Reed. He lives in Montreal.

Dorothée Bonnigal-Katz (translator) is a psychoanalyst based in London and Leamington Spa (West Midlands, UK). A member of The Site for Contemporary Psychoanalysis and the College of Psychoanalysts (UK), she is the founder and the clinical lead of the Psychosis Therapy Project at Islington Mind. She is a leading translator of psychoanalytic theory and philosophy. She has translated essays and books by Laurence Kahn, Jean Laplanche, Dominique Scarfone, Guy Rosolato, Pierre Legendre, Christopher Bollas and Miguel de Beistegui, among others.

Jonathan House (co-editor) is a psychiatrist and psychoanalyst in private practice. He teaches graduate seminars on the work of Freud and on the work of Laplanche at Columbia's Institute for Comparative Literature and Society. He is on the faculty and a Training and Supervising Analyst at Columbia's Psychoanalytic institute, The Center for Psychoanalytic Training and Research. A translator and an editor of translations from the French, he is the General Editor of The Unconscious in Translation. Initially appointed at the request of Jean Laplanche, he continues to be an active member of the Conseil Scientifique of Fondation Laplanche. A former Secretary of the American Psychoanalytic Association, he has served for many years on its Board of Directors.

Julie Slotnick (co-editor) studied comparative literature at Columbia University, Freie Universität Berlin, and Reid Hall, Columbia's Global Center in Paris. She works in New York as a freelance translator and editor.

Book design, Bill Schultz

A brief note on the history of The Unconscious In Translation

By Jonathan House, General Editor

The Unconscious In Translation LLC was first established in consultation with Jean Laplanche for the purpose of publishing a translation of *Sexual: La Sexualité élargie au sens freudien*. At that time, it was hoped that Johns Hopkins University Press would publish all of Laplanche's work. In 1976 Hopkins had published Jeffrey Mehlman's translation of Laplanche's "Life and Death in Psychoanalysis" (1970) and had kept it in print. Waiting for Hopkins to decide, Laplanche agreed that the completed translation of *Sexual* should be published. In addition, Laplanche and I agreed that UIT would publish the rest of his work in more or less reverse chronological order. In 2011, the translation of *Sexual* appeared with the title of "Freud and the *Sexual*". The work of translating that text, like the work involved in subsequent translations of Laplanche's work, received generous support from Fondation Laplanche.

Until 2012, UIT was an imprint of International Psychoanalytic Books (IPB). In 2012, UIT published "Brother of the Above", Donald Nicholson-Smith's translation of J.-B. Pontalis' *Frère du précédent* (which had won the Prix Médici Essai in 2006); and then UIT and IPB decided to work independently.

Since 2012, UIT has published:

"The Temptation of Biology: Freud's Theories of Sexuality, followed by Biologism and Biology" (2015) Donald Nicholson-Smith's translation of Laplanche's *Problématiques VII: Le Fourvoiement biologisant de la sexualité chez Freud*

"Laplanche: an introduction" (2015) by Dominique Scarfone which included not only Scarfone's 1997 text *Jean Laplanche* and Laplanche's 2010 "Preface to Beyond the Pleasure Principle", both translated by Dorothée Bonnigal-Katz, but also my new translation of the classic

1964 paper "Primal Fantasy, Fantasies of Origins, Origins of Fantasy" by Laplanche and Pontalis including the introduction the authors added in 1985.

In 2016 and 2017, in addition to this volume, The Unconscious in Translation will publish:

- *Problématiques VI: Après-coup*
- A new translation of Laplanche's "New Foundations for Psychoanalysis"
- *La Révolution copernicienne inachevée* – Laplanche's work from 1967-1992 other than that published in the series *Problématiques*
- Christophe Dejours' *Le Corps d'abord*
- Hélène Tessier's *Rationalisme et émancipation en psychanalyse: L'œuvre de Jean Laplanche*

UIT's books can be purchased on line at ucsintranslation.com